# Contents

KV-364-932

# Sustainable renewal of suburban areas

**Michael Gwilliam, Caroline Bourne**
*Civic Trust*

**Corinne Swain, Anna Prat**
*Ove Arup & Partners*

The **Joseph Rowntree Foundation** has supported this project as part of its programme of research and innovative development projects, which it hopes will be of value to policy makers and practitioners. The facts presented and views expressed in this report are, however, those of the authors and not necessarily those of the Foundation.

This research was conducted by the Civic Trust, working with Ove Arup & Partners

Published by YPS for the Joseph Rowntree Foundation

ISBN 1 902633 02 4

Prepared and printed by:
York Publishing Services Ltd
64 Hallfield Road
Layerthorpe
York YO31 7ZQ

# Acknowledgements

The Civic Trust is very grateful to the Joseph Rowntree Foundation for sponsoring this study, which was undertaken between April and August 1998. The Trust would also like to thank Bristol City Council, the London Borough of Redbridge, Birmingham City Council and North Tyneside Borough Council for their assistance in compiling the case studies and commenting on the draft. Finally, the Trust acknowledges the considerable assistance provided by their co-consultants Ove Arup and Partners and the members of the Advisory Panel.

# 1 Context

## Introduction

This document forms the Final Report of a pilot research study which has been developed by the Civic Trust in association with Ove Arup and Partners over the period April to August 1998. The original proposal for the study is set out in Appendix 1 to this report.

The project, which has been funded by the Joseph Rowntree Foundation, seeks to examine the opportunities for the contribution of suburban areas in the UK to achieving sustainable living measured in economic, social and environmental terms.

## Background to the project

Over recent years there has been a growing emphasis, in terms of both popular concern and public policy, on the need for sustainable regeneration and sustainability in Britain's urban areas. This trend has been sharpened recently by a vigorous debate about the capacity of existing towns and cities to accommodate a higher proportion of new housing demand, primarily because of concern about loss of countryside.

An underlying theme has been an increased concern for the quality of life in both urban and rural areas, both now and for future generations.

The various strands of current thinking are brought together in a number of studies carried out in the UK since 1995. The early work in Hertfordshire (Chesterton *et al.*, 1995) suggested that there might be considerable scope for increased development within existing urban areas. More recent work in, for example, the North-West region (Llewelyn-Davies, 1997) suggests that it is important to concentrate attention on specific areas of change, particularly on the fringes of commercial areas and near public transport nodes.

Particularly significant have been a series of studies for the London Planning Advisory Committee (LPAC).

- Potential residential capacity arising from conversion of surplus office space (*Office to other Uses*, London Property Research, October 1996).

- Potential for future housing growth through large-scale releases of land (*Future Sources of Large Scale Housing Land in London*, Halcrow Fox, February 1998).

- Capacity for new residential development through the promotion of the principles of sustainable residential quality on small sites (up to one hectare), on backland sites and through conversions of existing dwellings to flats (*Sustainable Residential Quality: New Approaches to Urban Living*, Llewelyn-Davies, January 1998).

- Nature of growth in expected numbers of single person households (*Housing Requirements of One Person*, P.S. Martin Hamlin, March 1998).

- Study of potential for additional dwellings in and over shops (*Dwellings Over and In Shops in London*, Civic Trust, August 1998).

The Joseph Rowntree Foundation has also supported a number of studies into housing capacity. As well as some work by the National Housing and Town Planning Council, this has notably included two studies by the Town and Country Planning Association (TCPA) at a regional level:

- *The People: Where Will They Go?* (TCPA, 1996)

- *Urban Housing Capacity: What Can Be Done?* (TCPA, 1998).

Although nominally addressing the whole urban area, the TCPA studies, and to an extent those for LPAC, have tended to concentrate on the scope for change within central and inner urban areas, on new development on the urban edge, or on new settlements.

The forthcoming guide on integrating sustainable development into the development plan process (Ove Arup and Partners, 1998) makes clear that it is important to examine how far the whole of the existing urban areas can be made more sustainable, and this includes the suburban areas where there may be opportunities to provide, for instance, improved public transport, a wider range of local facilities to reduce the need to travel, and a greater variety of housing stock.

The need for regeneration and renewal has also sparked a number of studies which have focused on the renewal of large municipal housing estates, much of this research funded by the Joseph Rowntree Foundation. In particular, researchers have been concerned with evaluating initiatives which have sought to re-build the physical environment as a contribution to social and economic concerns.

Many of the latter estates could be classed as 'suburban' in terms of their location and their relative dependency on a neighbouring metropolitan core. However, such estates are distinct from other suburban areas in terms of their origin and tenure and therefore present a distinct set of problems to address.

By way of contrast, we believe that relatively little work has been undertaken in the UK about the suburbs as a whole, and especially 'mixed use' or predominately privately owned suburbs, despite the fact that these suburbs make up a substantial part of the total housing stock.

## Rationale for research

It would appear that the apparent stability of much of suburbia may have meant that such areas have been somewhat overlooked in the quest for new opportunities in urban sustainability. With the clear focus of government policy on existing urban areas for housing and its quest for an 'urban renaissance' (J. Prescott, February 1998), the need to understand and assess the suburban discussion has aroused new importance. We need to understand their constraints and potentials better.

This pilot project seeks to examine a number of interrelated issues including:

- the changing definition of suburbia in the UK context

- the new pressures for change

- the opportunities for, and constraints on, the successful re-interpretation of the built form

- the avenues for intervention in suburban renewal

- examples of new options for more sustainable suburban patterns.

The aim of this study is to look at the ways in which suburban areas may need to adapt and may need to be helped to make that adaptation. Specifically, the research focuses on ways in which such areas can become more sustainable and so operate more effectively both in terms of their own populations and with respect to the larger urban areas of which they form such a significant part.

The central hypothesis of the research is based on the shared belief that there are particular locations within the suburbs which warrant specific attention, as offering 'scope for significant change'. Moreover, that there are certain areas which offer *more potential* than others for new forms of sustainable development. This study has tried to test this theory by attempting to identify new opportunities for 'sustainable suburbia', and to suggest means by which these opportunities might be realised.

# 2 Approach

## Introduction

There are a wide variety of urban areas which could be termed as 'suburban'. This study therefore begins by seeking to develop a *typology of suburbs*, focusing on current trends (and associated responses).

It should be emphasised that this project is seen as a forerunner for more in-depth research on the reinterpretation of the UK suburb. The resource limitations associated with this study have meant that case histories, in particular, are limited to a small selection of areas.

## Methodology

Despite the difficulties of precise definition and the scope for almost infinite variety, the term 'suburb' probably conjures up a similar picture for many people. For the most part it elicits images of predominantly residential, low rise, pre- and post-World War II developments, often devoid of the subtle mixture of uses and associated services which have gradually evolved in historic urban centres. This generality, however, masks a host of very different settlements with different origins and contrasting futures.

The first step was to explore the meaning and interpretation of the term 'suburb' in the British context. To do this has required an extensive literature review including a detailed analysis of international perspectives, in particular those from the US, Canada, Australia and mainland Europe. The different types of suburbs identified are discussed in Appendix 2. In addition, the team has pursued a number of structured interviews with leading academics and other professionals engaged in the development and renewal of urban Britain. The format for these interviews is set out in Appendix 3.

The secondary aim of the desktop research – as well as the structured interviews – has been to gain a clear understanding of the *catalysts for change*, as a basis for selecting case studies. The research, interviews and case studies all seek to address the following questions:

- Are there common trends (economic, social and policy-related) occurring within suburban areas as distinct from the main metropolitan core?

- How far are suburban areas sustainable?

- What models are being developed for achieving greater sustainability?

- To what extent can one differentiate between organic change and specific intervention in bringing about sustainable renewal in suburban areas?

- Are there key lessons in terms of specific initiatives or projects which can be adapted and imported to other areas?

Following definition of a typology and the principal catalysts we defined four examples of the main 'drivers' and selected four city suburbs where we could examine responses to change and the scope for more sustainable patterns of settlement and activity. These form the basis of the case studies.

The team also held Advisory Panel meetings hosted by the Joseph Rowntree Foundation to test out the original hypothesis, the selection of case studies and the preliminary findings. The membership of the Advisory Panel is set out in Appendix 4.

## Report structure

Chapters 1–5 set out the team approach to the brief, provide an overview of related research and put forward a suggested suburban typology. These chapters set the context within which the case studies were undertaken.

Chapter 6 sets out the methodology, and findings from the four case studies undertaken by the team can be found in Chapters 7 to 10.

Chapters 11 and 12 provide an overview of the research, conclusions and recommendations for action.

# 3  Defining 'suburbia'

## Introduction

In developing the rationale for this study, providing a simple definition of 'suburbia' or 'the suburbs' *per se* has proved rather difficult. Studies of the characteristics of the suburbs are few and far between in the UK and, while UK suburbs share some characteristics with those in North America and Northern Europe, the UK suburban experience has been shaped by a unique range of social, economic and political influences.

This section first examines literature on suburban development and trends in both the UK and overseas to create a context for the selected case studies. In the absence of detailed studies of the UK suburbs, we have sought to develop a new typology to define the suburban areas we found existed across the UK in the course of this study.

## General definition

The term 'suburb' is traditionally associated with a medium/low density residential area, with homes and gardens of similar size and type, adjacent to the city but dependent on it for employment, services and trade. The origin of the name itself implies its main characteristic, namely its subordinate position to a town (from the Latin *sub urbs*). A suburb does not usually have a full set of urban functions and is not a self-contained urban system on its own. The type of urban area on which it depends is usually a large town or a metropolis. The larger the town, the more vast the suburban ring around it and the greater the subtle differentiation of types of suburban areas.

Suburbs have always existed. In every period, the part of the town called suburb has represented a peripheral stage in urban expansion and population dispersion. The nature and status of that suburb has, however, varied enormously. There are accounts, for example, of suburban developments in Mesopotamian cities and in the Middle Ages (Mumford, 1961) which were inhabited by the more wealthy members of the community, who, in times of peace, could afford to live at a distance from the centre. Conversely, the medieval suburbs described by Geoffrey Chaucer in the *Canterbury Tales* in 1386 were slums just outside the town walls.

Mass suburbanisation is, however, essentially a phenomenon of the last two centuries. The modern form of suburb, designed to provide the habitat for the average Western household, is the result of massive industrialisation, urban population growth, transport innovations and changes in lifestyle. Industrialisation – and successively the growth of service and public sectors – has created the potential and the desire for separating home from workplace. Population growth created a substantial demand for new housing for the working and middle classes. Finally, transport innovations have made commuting from a long distance possible.

By and large, suburban growth initially represented an ameliorative exodus from slum conditions which characterised many early industrial towns. Following these pioneering and often planned suburban expansions, suburbanisation has grown exponentially and become the main form of town expansion. Recently some commentators have argued that suburbanisation has now given way to forms of de-urbanisation towards the smaller centres outside larger towns or to the opposite trend of selective re-urbanisation of town centres (Hall and Hay, 1980; van den Berg *et al.*, 1982; Cheshire and Hay, 1989).

Suburbs are also the result of a so-called Anglo-Saxon 'planning ideology', which has promoted the image of a pastoral garden suburb suitable for families with children. The planning background in Britain (Ebenezer Howard, etc.) and the United States share the 'garden suburb' model, which is usually attributed to Britain but had also some early American influences. This aspiration to an urban model which is both decentralised but with a strong sense of community is still an ideal for many.

The basic element of these developments – the suburban house – represents the 'collective urban form of the country house' (Mumford, 1961). This house-type is seen as an essential element of a post-war society, inasmuch as it is the ideal shelter for a traditional nuclear family where one adult is commuting and working downtown and the other shopping and taking care of the house and children locally. This type of family is probably no longer representative of a typical suburban household, but the type of housing has not changed.

Although the suburbs have proved a popular form of mass housing, the environmental consequences of suburbs are now under discussion.

## International comparisons

Historically, the UK experience of suburban development is very similar to the American one. Models of suburban development have crossed the Atlantic in both directions – just as other social and economic developments have.

In the *United States, Australia and Canada*, suburbia has often been seen as a materialisation of a primarily post-war social dream (the 'American dream') and has remained a prevalent consumer preference with more Americans now living in the suburbs than in rural or central areas (45 per cent of the metropolitan US population are now living in the suburbs according to the 1990 Census). Suburbs are 'the symbol and logos of American affluence and technology and growth in the past 40 years' (Van der Ryn and Calthorpe, 1986, p. 34).

In terms of sustainability, however, it has been argued that the American model of suburbia, with its low density sprawling housing estates, often total car dependency and little in the way of community facilities, is the worst kind of urban structure (Angotti, 1993). Walker (1981) expressed concern that this housing typology leads to an atomised and individualistic style of life which does not help community development, and which

is unsuitable in its high consumption of land and energy for transport.

There have been many studies identifying cases of social fragmentation in the suburbs as ethnically and socially similar neighbourhoods have developed, with the most extreme case being the socially regressive 'gated community' in which non-residential and 'non-compatible' social groups are banned. Downs (1973) states that this process has left behind difficult social situations in the inner city, creating a fundamentally unjust and segregated society. A more socially balanced suburb, which integrates a range of social and ethnic groups, is likely to create a more sustainable place in which to live and work.

The characteristics of different suburban areas in the USA are aided by a high level of localised fiscal autonomy from the adjacent inner areas and city centre. The way in which local politicians influence spending has had a major impact on the social and community status of individual suburbs. This is a crucial difference between America and the UK, where in the latter the focus of much local spending is decided nationally and suburban autonomy has been held much more in check.

Cultural perceptions of suburbia differ in *Continental Northern Europe* where, unlike the UK or US, town or city centre apartments are favoured above suburban dwellings. Suburban housing on the Continent tends to be synonymous with large public housing estates. Further, the Continental Northern European experience, although not homogenous, differs from the USA in terms of:

- the greater role of the public sector

- the relative strength of the private housing market

- the need to respond to limitations of space

- different patterns of urban lifestyle and cultural networks.

In Northern Europe, suburban areas have often been planned as decentralised dormitory poles, with their own local services and shops and good public transport connections with the town centre. The most famous example of this multi-centred model of planning is Stockholm, which, in 50 years of planning policies, has shaped itself in clusters around an efficient rail system (Cervero, 1995). This example counters a view that economic wealth is always coupled with dispersal and car-led forms of developments. Freiburg is another example of rising living standards but static car ownership, and a very strong suburban public transport and development pattern (Pucher and Clorer, 1992; see also Newman *et al.*, 1995).

Public housing intervention in the northern European social democracies has also had a major impact on the shape and social characteristics of many suburbs. The social housing enclaves built by the French Government, such as the Habitation à Loyer Modéré, have become the focus of the most difficult urban problems and a priority in urban policy. Urban policy in Continental Europe has focused very much on these peripheral estates. In some cases, buildings have been demolished, in others they have been refurbished – such as in the successful case of Vällingby in Sweden.

The resulting suburban landscape is extremely varied, ranging from individual leafy housing estates, to small apartment blocks with a stronger visual urban connotation, to high rise modernist buildings in distressed peripheral enclaves.

With the exception of the public housing estates, suburban areas in Northern Europe tend to be more socially mixed than American counterparts, with more stable communities, closely linked to employment areas. They have also adopted a significantly closer development pattern and normally a reasonably comprehensive network of public transport services. This is due in part to the lower population mobility and the rigidity of the housing market. However, this scenario may change with the rise of gated, single-class commuter communities, as has happened recently around Paris or in places such as Milano 2, in Northern Italy.

## The UK experience: types of suburbs

The UK suburbs share aspects of development history with both North America and Continental Northern Europe. In common with the US, the UK suburbs shared early aspirations to the ideal of the 'garden city', whereas, in aspects of public sector involvement and spatial constraints on development, the UK shares more similarities with Continental Europe.

The history of the UK suburbs is of particular interest to this study, as it throws up different typologies responding to different needs and attracting different social groupings. The suburb is a multi-faceted spatial concept, which changes in relation to location and over time. Just like changing patterns of urban expansion, the qualities of suburban developments have also changed significantly.

Developing typologies of suburbs has been a popular academic exercise in the US. For example, David Thorns (1972) identified eight categories crossing working class and middle class types of suburb with four categories: planned residential, unplanned residential, planned industrial, unplanned industrial. Schnore (1963) has added a category for mixed usage. Other authors such as Schneider and Fernandez (1989) distinguish between booming, declining, transformation and production-based suburbs. Muller (1976), following a popular categorisation, recognised four types of suburbs: exclusive upper income suburbs; middle-class family suburbs; suburban cosmopolitan centres and working-class suburbs. New terms have even been created such as 'exurb', to indicate new forms of suburban, upper-middle class settlements in semi-rural areas (Spectorsky, 1957).

Drawing on our experience, we were able to identify six types of British suburbs. The 'historic inner suburb', 'the planned suburb', 'the social housing suburb' and 'the suburban town' were identified as typologies representing particular building styles or notable historic stages in development of urban areas. Detailed descriptions of this type of suburban area can be found in Appendix 2.

The 'public transport suburb' and the 'car suburb' are more general distinctions, within which most suburban developments in the UK fit. These represent the 'average' suburbs either built in close proximity to a significant public transport node, or spread out assuming access by car.

Table 1 presents a summary of the qualities of these types. In the remainder of this chapter we focus on the two 'average' types of suburb in the UK. A more extensive description of the origin and qualities of the other types can be found in Appendix 2.

The *public transport suburb* was the main type of the first half of the twentieth century expansion of many metropolitan areas in Britain and around the world. The outer ring of London from eight to 15 miles from the centre was largely the product of transportation changes. The expansion of the railway lines into the countryside and the tram and bus network made it possible for private and public developers to accommodate a fast growing population (2,000,000 additional people in London from 1911 to 1931). In the majority of cases, developers followed the railways; in other cases, such as in Bexley, they anticipated them (Jackson, 1973, p. 167). The same happened in Manchester, Birmingham, Newcastle, Glasgow and the rest of Britain, although in different periods because of the immigration processes brought about by the depression.

### Table 1 Types of suburbs

| Type | Characteristics | Examples |
|------|-----------------|----------|
| Historic inner suburb | Established terraced or semi-detached developments now integrated to the rest of town; urban qualities, e.g. mix of uses, 'walkability', good public transport | Clapham, London |
| Planned suburb | Few enclaves now absorbed into the rest of town; usually successful | Bourneville, Birmingham |
| Social housing suburb | High or low rise housing estates often with problems of maintenance, safety, vandalism, lack of social mix and non-residential uses | St Helier, Sutton |
| Suburban town | Suburbs acquiring urban village functions for a wider sub-metropolitan area | Croydon |
| Public transport suburb | Medium density homogenous speculative suburbs, usually in a closely structured urban fabric | Ruislip, Middlesex |
| Car suburb | Low density, detached housing, homogenous speculative suburbs, often in an 'open' townscape fringe area (motorways, out of town shopping centres and golf clubs) | Bushey Heath, Hertsmere |

The public transport suburbs were designed for everyone – from council tenants, blue and white collars, professionals and managers, to war heroes – but were often divided by class. The outer suburban ring of London included various types of suburbs ranging from spacious and leafy settlements, such as Chislehurst and Ealing; to middle-class suburbs on the low-fare Great Northern Railway, such as Bowes Park, Palmers Green, Wood Green, Hornsey, Crouch End; to suburbs for artisans and clerks, such as Tottenham, Edmonton, Walthamstow and Leyton (Jackson, 1973, p. 1).

Despite differences, the mass result of this trend has been the growth of a more or less uniform 'semi-detached London' (Jackson, 1973) – and by extension 'semi-detached Britain'. Within each area, variety of tenure and types of housing are very low. The predominant housing type offered is 'good, cheap, basic housing with gardens for people who could never earlier have aspired to anything like it' (Hall, 1989, p. 20). Density was usually set around 10–12 houses/acre. There was little interest in integrating this residential expansion with office and industrial uses. Shops created the only variety in this landscape but were systematically concentrated in designated street parades relating to the stations.

The *car suburb*, which succeeded the public transport suburb after the World War II, filled the interstices not originally covered by public transport. The housing types are not substantially different from those of the railway suburbs. Density can be lower, down to even levels of four houses/acre or less. Car-dominated spaces determine the form of these developments, especially in terms of car parking and road layout, with garages and wide streets.

The public transport and car suburbs, which occupy large areas of the British town, have been seen as problematic since the time of Abercrombie's 1944 Greater London Plan. Frequently they have been accused of being one of the less inspiring type

of urban settlement. More recently Peter Hall has noted that:

> The suburbs will not last for ever. In the late 1980s, they are between 50 and 70 years old. Not all were well built; not all have been well maintained. The cost of maintaining them will surely rise, and their owners may not be able to meet it. Some may well degenerate into new slums, and the question of clearance and rebuilding will then loom large. (Hall, 1989, p. 20)

## The UK experience compared

The suburban experience in the UK represents a middle way between the American and European model. Here we present the main similarities and differences.

- *Suburban aspiration*: in the UK, suburbs grew as a result of a middle-class rejection of inner city living. This has happened in Continental Europe as well, but the aspiration to an arcadian, single-use area, single-family house lifestyle is more developed in the Anglo-Saxon world than in Continental Europe. Builders in Britain would argue that suburbs, as they have been so far, are what the market demands.

- *Housing types*: the individual house model in Britain and the US, Australia and Canada have broad similarities. Individual family, cottage, neo-traditional types have always been popular. In addition, the existence of a more concentrated volume house building industry in Britain has fostered the reproduction of standardised housing types and patterns of town expansion.

- *Car dependence, land use and density*: car dependence in the UK has steadily increased and extensive fringe/motorway suburban landscapes have recently appeared. Despite this, British suburbia is still more compact and denser than its American counterparts. Development land in the UK is expensive. However, the degree of compactness and mix of uses is significantly lower than Continental suburban areas.

- *Social nature and community*: the UK flight to the suburbs shares many characteristics with the American experience (see earlier in this chpater), aggravating inner-city problems, but to a lesser degree. On average, British suburbs are not usually associated with the high level of social problems of the many distressed Continental European peripheries where the term 'suburb' is generally associated with unpopular public housing estates which often share the social problems of British and American inner cities. Finally, the 'engulfed villages' within British

metropoles provide an important opportunity to build local distinctiveness, community participation and identity around a historic core, which cannot be found easily in the US, Australia and Canada.

- *Politics and policies*: Britain has also been for the last 20 years more centralised in terms of government than the USA and the majority of European countries. Suburban authorities do not have strong means to determine their future independently from the main town. They have a lower level of political and fiscal autonomy, which affects the scope of their local policies and actions. Innovative approaches to suburban renewal, which can be found in the USA and in some cases in Continental Europe, may therefore be more difficult to achieve.

# 4 Sustainability and suburban development

## Defining a sustainable settlement

Recent years have seen a growing literature seeking to define the qualities of sustainable development. This has grown out of the work done by the Brundtland Commission and spread into many fields and disciplines. Sustainable urban development – management, growth and renewal – has emerged as a key field of research and policy.

A sustainable settlement should be as much as possible inherently sustainable at neighbourhood, town and regional level, and also contribute to the achievement of global sustainable development.

> *A sustainable city is one in which its people and businesses continuously endeavour to improve their natural, built and cultural environments at neighbourhood and regional levels, whilst working in ways which always support the goal of global sustainable development.* (Haughton and Hunter, 1994, p. 27)

The forthcoming guide on integrating sustainable development into planning (Ove Arup and Partners, 1998) provides an outline for developing sustainable proposals for urban areas and for assessing how far these meet sustainable objectives. This guide and other sources (e.g. European Commission, 1996; CAG, 1997) stress the importance of involving local communities (including businesses and investors) in the decision making about change. In particular this is seen as important in terms of enabling local communities to identify the deficits in their community, so that changes address the particular needs of the area and are more likely to result in long-term practicable improvements, supported by local people.

There are three types of objectives suggested by the Arup guide and by others (e.g. CAG, 1997) as being important:

- *Economic sustainability*: establishing a robust economy, with a wide range of employment and development opportunities, and maintaining the vitality and viability of town and village centres.

- *Social sustainability*: improving the quality of life, reducing inequalities in access to key features which are identified as priorities in contributing to quality of life, and achieving social cohesion, security and safety.

- *Environmental sustainability*: reducing levels of waste and emissions (including those from vehicles), and protecting and enhancing non-renewable resources including land, ecological, historical and cultural heritage.

The guide suggests that it is vital to have a clear vision of what sustainable neighbourhoods should be like. Specifically they should have:

- an identified centre focused on public transport nodes normally comprising shopping, a mix of community-based services, higher density housing, and easily reached from residential areas by foot and cycle

- areas of higher density residential development close to the centre which will help to support the range of services, and will have low car usage because of those services which are close by

- their own distinctive character which reflects their history, topography and landscape, and the range and type of housing and related development.

## Sustainability and the renewal of suburbia

While the problems associated with inner cities have received great attention in terms of government intervention and investment, many suburban areas have, conversely, suffered from under-investment. Such areas are not seen as priorities and are rarely applicable for urban programme funding. Consequently, they are left to

11

contend by themselves against decline and environmental degradation. It is true that some of them are successful but, even in these cases, the environmental and social costs of this type of urban development have traditionally been under-estimated.

Increasingly suburban areas have come under attack from critics across a range of issues:

> ... the failure of the periphery: the absence of public life, the paucity of culture, the visual monotony, the time wasted in commuting. By contrast the city offers density and variety; the efficient time- and energy-saving combination of social and economic functions. (European Community, 1990, p. 19)

The suburb is largely antithetical to such concepts as self-sufficiency and containment, energy efficiency and community enterprise. It is – as its name suggests – dependent on core functions located elsewhere within the urban system. This symbiosis is increasingly associated with a number of distinct problems in terms of sustainability.

### Economic sustainability

Economically, suburban areas are characterised by dependence on a separate centre for employment opportunities and for associated facilities including retail and leisure uses. There is usually a shortage or lack of non-residential uses. When productive or commercial uses do exist they are usually highly zoned. Complete economic self-containment may not be achievable – and probably not desirable as an end in itself – but the current situation produces a series of non-sustainable consequences.

Since suburbs are not self-contained, they require relevant flows of people and resources to support them. This dependence on external resources and facilities generates traffic and consequently energy consumption and pollution. There is little information available to illustrate this job/resident balance for suburban areas because of the problems of definition of boundaries. Average work trip length data are not published below

district level. However, evidence suggests that the residents of more suburbanised areas do have longer average work journeys, e.g. Surrey Heath 14.6 km compared to Watford 8.8 km (Ove Arup and Partners, 1998).

The low level of economic self-dependence also means that suburbs are too frequently vulnerable to external economic changes. Their capability to re-structure themselves endogenously may vary significantly from area to area. In some cases, the weakness of social and community networks, which results from the commuting nature of the local population and the lower density, does not help to absorb crises. Residents who can will simply choose to leave the area and this will aggravate the process of decline. In other cases, the strength of suburban community links can make the difference.

### Social sustainability

Suburbs can be prone to social specialisation. This is mainly because of the available housing types, their tenure and cost, service provision and accessibility which tend to exclude some groups by age, income, family structure, mobility, ethnicity. This is not in accord with sustainability principles. It is, however, also the case that some suburbs demonstrate considerable social stability and a well developed sense of community.

In many older suburbs there is evidence of recent loss of facilities. Community services, for example, have been increasingly centralised, and new shopping investment has been focused on the existing cores or has moved out of town. Lower Earley provides a recent example of how many private sector suburbs have developed, usually over a concentrated period of time, to serve particular housing demand (predominantly three bedroom houses with gardens), and with poorly co-ordinated provision of services (Arup and Partners, 1998).

The heavy reliance on the car as a means of transport has also served to marginalise sections of the population who do not have access to this facility. Social polarisation has tended to increase as a result. In addition the lack of pedestrian movement reduces social contacts and slows down processes of community building.

### Environmental sustainability

In ecological terms, suburban living is associated with a range of 'unsustainable' features including: high levels of car dependency, above-average energy consumption and relatively high land consumption, reflecting low densities. The reliance

on the private motor car in particular has led to growing concerns over congestion, air quality, noise and public safety on roads. Related data analysis is frustrated by boundary problems, but, nonetheless, evidence suggests that higher car usage is a feature of suburbanised lower density areas (Newman and Kenworthy, 1989).

There is the perception that suburban areas can provide a monotonous physical environment with a lack of distinctive character, particularly where the centre is not based on a historic core. The quality of a traditional city, defined by Ward (1989)

**Figure 4.1 Images of suburbia**

**Table 2  Problems of sustainability in suburban areas**

| | Problems |
|---|---|
| **Economic** | Economic dependence on external employment and commercial areas and facilities – lack of self-containment and lack of economic base variety. Low level of investment in older suburbs. |
| **Social** | *Social community participation/identity* |
| | Often social specialisation. In some cases, lack of sense of identity and sense of belonging. High resident turnover in some public housing estates, which could undermine social cohesion. |
| | *Quality of life/culture/social vitality and mix* |
| | Mainly residential uses; lack of community focus. Insufficient and poorly accessible shops. Low level of social and cultural vitality. Limited household variety and social mix. |
| **Environmental** | *Ecology and natural environment* |
| | Consumption of land and energy. Car dependence; with lack of alternative transport choices. Congestion, speed of traffic and rat-running problems. |
| | *Quality of the built environment* |
| | 'Ugliness' of sprawl. Lack of continuity of the urban fabric, distinctiveness, permeability and fine grain. Unsafe and neglected public spaces. Housing decay in older suburbs. |

as its fine grain, which, despite its complexity, is transparent and recognisable to the user, is exactly what is lacking in many modern suburban developments. Design literature is full of criticism of the quality of urban design in suburbia, creating a lack of identity.

Low density and mediocre design can also result in a poor delineation of the boundary between town and country, creating problems of trespass and disturbance which are difficult to manage.

Some of the literature is, however, too critical. Only some authors (e.g. Southworth and Owens, 1993) have taken a more balanced view. There are many suburban areas in the UK that are popular,

attractive, enjoy a reasonable level of facilities and have a strong sense of community. They will also probably show characteristics such as low density and car dependency which are unsustainable, but the picture is grey rather than black and their positive qualities should be recognised. Our point is simply that most suburbs exhibit a number of relatively unsuitable characteristics, and that the scope to improve their *relative* sustainability therefore deserves to be explored.

Table 2 is a summary of the problems which can be found in suburban areas and which undermine their sustainability in economic, social and environmental terms.

Figure 4.2 Southworth's analysis of suburban forms (USA) (reproduced by permission of the *Journal of the American Planning Association* and the authors, Michael Southworth and Peter Owens, *The Evolving Metropolis, JAPA*, Vol. 59, issue no. 3, Summer 1993)

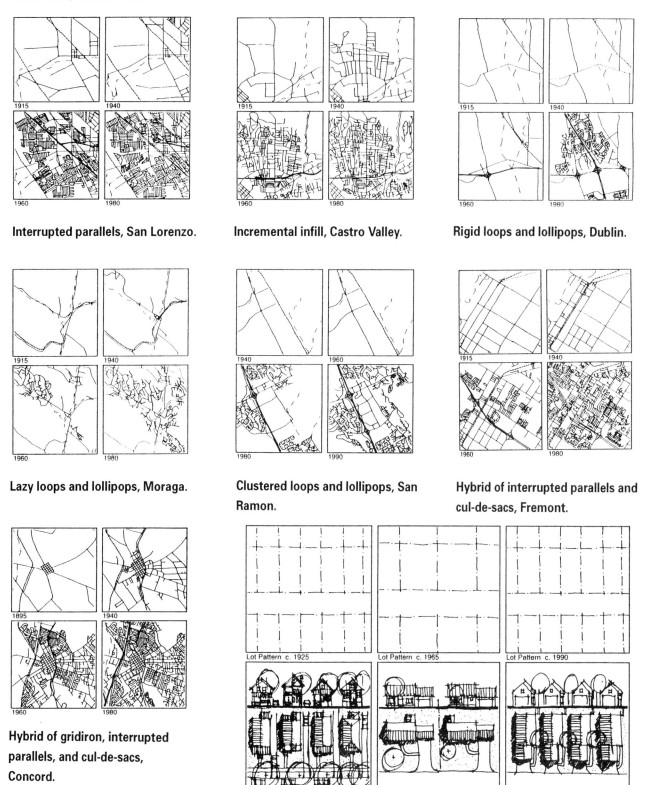

Interrupted parallels, San Lorenzo.

Incremental infill, Castro Valley.

Rigid loops and lollipops, Dublin.

Lazy loops and lollipops, Moraga.

Clustered loops and lollipops, San Ramon.

Hybrid of interrupted parallels and cul-de-sacs, Fremont.

Hybrid of gridiron, interrupted parallels, and cul-de-sacs, Concord.

Lot and building patterns.

# 5 New models for sustainable suburbs

## Introduction

Urban planners, environmentalists, architects and local authorities have recently started to focus their attention on mechanisms to reduce the lack of sense of community and placelessness, visual monotony, car dependence, energy consumption, single use and single class character of many suburbs.

It is difficult to draw neat theoretical lines between these models and it is not the purpose of this exercise. Often many elements from transport, design, management, social aspects and ecology are mixed together. In addition, this literature usually focuses on new developments. Here we review it briefly to see how these emerging concepts can be applied to sustainable renewal of existing suburban areas and consider some experiences on the ground.

## New urbanism, small town America and city plans

In the US, the 'new urbanism' and the 'small town America' approach (Katz, 1992) grew up from the belief that 'many people feel a loss of place and a loss of community in the American landscape' (Foxworthy, 1997). The environmental and social costs of sprawl have become unacceptable. Jacobs (1961), who is considered the founder mother of this movement, identified the quality of economically successful, culturally vibrant and environmentally pleasant towns in the intricate web of human relationships built in space over time. An urban environment with this quality allows for casual public contact in lively streets, variety of uses, density of people and cultures, meaningful public spaces and identifiable neighbourhoods.

As seen in Chapter 3, the American suburbs have often been accused of being just the opposite. Awareness is growing that they need to be re-interpreted as self-sustaining urban entities with 'the qualities of community design which establish diversity, pedestrian scale and public identity' (Calthorpe, 1993, p. 3). This re-interpretation has been done in the US at two different levels, either in terms of urban design (or so-called 'suburban surgery' at the development level), or in terms of management and community issues at the neighbourhood or town level.

Related literature has built on the desire to recreate 'small town America' or 'traditional neighbourhood designs' (Duany and Plater-Zyberk, 1991). Following this approach, many experiments have taken place. The re-development of Stapleton in Denver, led by the non-profit Stapleton Re-development Foundation, aims at creating a sustainable working model, based on neighbourhood units, green frameworks and neo-traditional design elements, in an existing, very unsustainable suburban area (Brown, 1985).

In some cases the same design-oriented thinking has been applied to improve existing suburban areas, such as in Sandy Springs in Georgia, a 'suburban surgery' realised by HOH Associates where revitalisation has focused on the 1950s strip (Lindgren, 1995). Many of these schemes take advantage of the opportunities offered by voids in the suburban fabric to create greater continuity, a finer urban grain, higher density and mix of uses.

Other experiences have focused on comprehensive town-wide plans and community aspects. These exercises aim at creating a vision and framework for future development and renewal decisions, without being as prescriptive and specific as a town plan. The Vancouver City Plan promotes a city of neighbourhoods and stresses the importance of local participation (City of Vancouver, 1995). Bellevue was a vast nondescript suburb of Seattle, before a new set of zoning, transport, development incentives for mixed use and cultural facilities, and design regulations were devised to transform the whole character of the area (Hinshaw, 1989). Portland's 'Liveable City

Programme' has proved to be a very successful strategy to reduce urban sprawl in a fast-growing area, and improve the environmental and social qualities of existing neighbourhoods (City of Portland, 1993). Similarly, variously called liveable neighbourhood initiatives have been set in place in many Californian cities.

The application of these experiences to the renewal of suburbs in the UK requires a degree of adaptation. Two aspects would have to be considered: on the one side, the different nature of the British suburban landscape; on the other, the different institutional arrangements, fiscal powers and level of autonomy of local authorities. However, there are important lessons to be learned, especially in terms of the need to involve local communities in the process of creating a vision and defining change in suburban areas.

## European urban village and compact city

Other recent models of urban development have focused on density and mix of uses. The traditional European medium-size city is often taken as the ideal model of sustainable urban life (Montgomery, 1998). The 'urban villages' and 'compact city' literature can be broadly related to this model. The urban model is based on medium/high density, mix of uses, social mix within the same area and individual buildings, public transport and walkability, local distinctiveness created by referring to historic urban and architectural forms. This vision goes beyond the neighbourhood to the wider urban dimension.

The Urban Villages Forum argues the case for a human scale, mixed use, design quality approval to development and re-development whether in the inner city or the suburb (Aldous, 1992). Leon Krier has applied these thoughts to the creation of a neo-traditional suburb in Poundbury in Dorchester. Most 'urban villages' work has, however, been applied to new schemes or individual estates.

In terms of renewal of suburban areas, the 'urban villages' approach suggests – implicitly or explicitly – the scope to re-develop some sites, increase densities and design a varied and high quality community environment.

*Instead of continuing to densify historical centres beyond their physical and social capacity and of feeding more and more open countryside to the expanding suburbs, I believe that many suburban areas offer a high potential for future development.*
(L. Krier quoted in Aldous, 1992)

In some European countries officials are now looking to remodel suburban areas, which were originally designed following the functionalist principles of zoning and car transport based on motorways, and to create more compact cities. The Netherlands in particular is very much committed in this direction. For example, in the 1960s suburb of Bijlmermeer in Amsterdam, the transport corridors and their related buffer zones will be re-developed following a compact city model, with higher densities and houses closer to the major roads. Significantly, the notion of the 'compact city' has been espoused by the European Commission (1990) and is being reflected in the current development of major European Union urban initiatives and programmes.

These experiences could in time be applicable to the renewal of suburbs in the UK, but the concept is at present too recent a development to allow many conclusions to be drawn.

## Linkage and mobility

Transport and mobility are crucial issues in the sustainable renewal of suburbs. Car dependence has drawbacks in terms of environmental impact (noise, pollution, energy consumption), accessibility for less mobile people, and the level of physical interaction and exchange between people. Many new urban models, whether called

17

'pedestrian pocket' or 'transit oriented Development', are now focusing on re-creating suburbs where car dependence is reduced. They represent the modern re-interpretation of the railway suburbs.

The 'pedestrian pocket' approach specifically seeks to create a walkable neighbourhood centre, which can become the heart of the community (Untermann, 1984; Kelbaugh, 1989). In terms of design, much work has been done on how to improve street layout in order to avoid the dominance of cars and car-related spaces. In the States such projects do not challenge general car dependency, but seek to create areas of car exclusion. Similar initiatives have been pioneered in the UK context with recent examples including the car-free zones in Edinburgh.

The 'transit-oriented development' (TOD) is a model connected with the 'new urbanism' movement (described above). Laguna West, an 800 acre new development site in Sacramento, California, has been designed by Calthorpe and Associates, according to a model of a mixed used community within an average of 2,000 feet walking distance of the station and the centre. In this context, suburban congestion is also a growing problem which is now starting to be addressed (Cervero, 1986).

In Europe – especially in Germany, Switzerland, The Netherlands and the Nordic countries – pedestrianisation, the creation of networks of cycle- and pathways, massive promotion of public transport and limitation of car use have been widely promoted. Clearly such initiatives, while not specific to the suburbs, can play a significant role in facilitating lifestyle changes in such areas and creating more attractive neighbourhoods, with less car dependency and less noise and air pollution.

While improving internal linkage may have had some effect on promoting a shift to more environmentally friendly transport modes, it has not led to a re-interpretation of the suburb in terms of settlement pattern. Links to the core are more critical in this respect. Clearly, improving the accessibility of core functions can have a number of very different implications. On the one hand it can reinforce the inherent dependency of the suburb on the core. However, it can also provide the vital catalyst for the introduction of new land uses and new densities in suburban areas.

## Eco-towns and eco-suburbs

'Eco-towns', with substantially lower impacts on the environment and in terms of resources consumption, have now been built around the world. Review of these experiments suggests how the same thinking could be applied to improve existing suburban areas.

Village Homes in California is a community where residents grow 90 per cent of their food on communal land and every house is solar panelled. Ecolonia in The Netherlands is the result of a bold strategy which combines land use, services, resources conservation, housing design and transport in a sustainable way. The ecological community of Halifax in South Australia provides evidence that these principles can be implemented coherently even in very suburban contexts. An ecologically-sound suburb has been developed in Örebro in Sweden with extensive measures for water and waste management, composting, allotments, solar collectors, green shops and jointly-owned cars (Heidemij, 1995). Some UK local authorities, such as Leicester City Council, when facing the need to intervene on decaying housing stocks, now consider strategies to increase energy efficiency. In Bradford, residents have worked with designers to turn the land of an ex-housing estate into a site producing food for the community.

These or similar measures could be adopted in existing suburban areas. A comprehensive programme of eco-measures may be difficult and expensive to put in place in an already built area, but packages of improvements in energy conservation and efficiency, water and waste management, transport and green areas could be relatively easily introduced. It may be argued that these changes are relatively expensive in comparison to the local economic benefits they produce. However, the case of energy efficiency improvements in Leicester has demonstrated that they generate substantial benefits to the community in terms of sense of belonging, care for the local facilities and environment, and reduction of crime.

## Sustainable city regions and communities

Economic and social aspects of the suburbs are critical if any renewal initiative is to be effective and lasting. This means going beyond purely physical aspects and considering traffic and population flows, strengths and weaknesses of the local economy, characteristics of the local communities and their needs, property and land values, housing tenures, types and market change.

Breheny (1993) and Lock (1994) enlarge the discussion on urban sustainability by looking at the sustainable city region. Suburban areas are affected by urban decentralisation and regionalisation. In this context, compacting the city may not always be the solution. Renewal can be achieved by major interventions and re-organisation of the regional space or by innovatory development patterns. Using local potential and increasing physical connections between localities are key instruments.

The social and community aspects are frequently emphasised as essential components of a comprehensive renewal strategy at both regional and local level. The most famous example of such a strategy was the regeneration of Oak Park in Chicago in the 1970s (Godwin, 1979). The area, close to the deprived West Side Ghetto, was under risk of serious decline of housing and social conditions accompanied – as often happens in the US – by racial turnover. This scenario was prevented as the result of a strong bottom-up community approach to face social and racial

integration and allow people to remain on site. Outside real estate firms were discouraged from promoting panic selling. Local residents controlled schools and local services. Local government funding provided low interest loans to re-model existing housing. The Ford Foundation gave its help to control property values.

## Summary

There is no one way to re-interpret the suburb. The various models presented above are a combination of different elements. Each renewal strategy has to be tailored to the local opportunities and constraints, and to local pressures for change. This is the subject of the next chapter. As a summary, however, here is a list of the elements which should be considered in a renewal strategy for appropriate suburbs:

- **increased mix of uses**

- **re-design of suburban centres**

- **re-development of brownfield sites or urban voids**

- **selective densification of housing**

- **sustainable transport (especially buses, cycle and pedestrian networks)**

- **regional planning (connecting the suburb to a polycentric urban system)**

- **participation and community involvement**

- **more positive and creative urban design guidance**

- **environmental and green space improvement**

- **housing maintenance, improvement and mix of tenure and types**

- **more efficient and accessible facilities and public services.**

19

Figure 5.1  The urban village approach to change in an existing suburb (reproduced with the kind permission of the Urban Villages Forum: *Urban Villages Report* first published by the Urban Villages Group, 1992)

**Right: 80-acre (33-hectare) area of a typical suburb devoid of all but residential accommodation.**

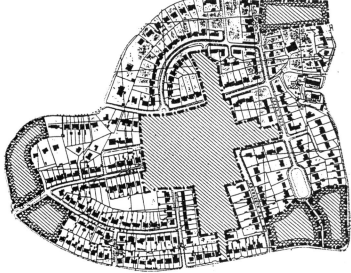

**Left: 10–20 acres (4–8 hectares) forming the geographical centre of the proposed urban village and up to 10 acres (4 hectares) at the periphery are declared Urban Re-development Areas**

**Right: Over a period of 10–15 years the designated Re-development Areas are transformed into an urban village integrating all the required uses, services and workplaces. Large employers and schools are located in the large peripheral lots in courtyard buildings.**

**Figure 5.2  Site plan for the Halifax EcoCity, Adelaide, Australia (reproduced with permission from *Town & Country Planning*, January 1997, p. 27)**

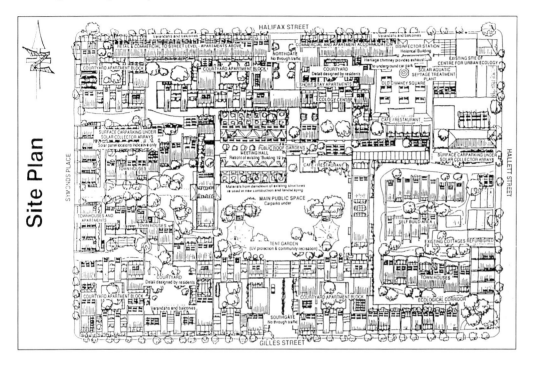

# 6 Opportunities for change

## Introduction

Suburbs are generally perceived to be one of the most stable parts of urban areas. This has certainly been the perception until recently in America in the writings of such as Statura (1987). In the UK, town planners have concentrated on the problems and opportunities of inner urban areas and former industrial zones.

This perception of limited potential for change in the suburban areas has, however, recently been potentially clarified by the urban capacity studies carried out to investigate how far it might be possible to provide in urban areas for the 4.4 million additional households identified in the most recent projections (Llewelyn-Davies, 1997; Ove Arup and Partners, 1998). Despite the early expectations (Chesterton *et al.*, 1995), the studies suggest that many suburban areas of towns have limited scope for physical change in the short term. The findings can be summarised as follows.

- Many, though not all, suburbs have tended to be developed over short periods with similar types of housing, so that there is not the range of age or type of building stock to enable re-development or adaptation of older buildings.

- There is a multiplicity of private ownerships, particularly (though now not only) on the private estates, making land assembly more difficult.

- There can be a strong resistance to change from local residents who often place a high value on the environment which they have bought.

- In some suburbs there may be lack of open spaces making their protection and extension an important element in the improvement of the quality of life in the area.

In these circumstances the capacity studies have tended to concentrate on the more obvious areas of transition on the fringes of the main commercial centres, on the potential of the larger brownfield or re-development sites, and on the design needs of higher density new development.

Our analysis, nevertheless, suggests there are pressures for change in some suburban areas that may provide the opportunity for renewal, related to a clear vision of how the area may function more sustainably in economic, social and environmental terms. From our earlier analysis and consultation, we have identified four main drivers of such change, although there may well be others:

- *Local investment*: suburban areas may be the recipients of substantial new public or private investment, whether related to infrastructure, provision of facilities, or commercial development.

- *Rationalisation of provision*: suburbs have been particularly affected by changes in operation of commercial and service providers, with the loss of retailing, health and social facilities.

- *Local involvement*: local community initiatives such as Agenda 21, and the efforts towards devolution in local government, provide opportunities for suburban communities to take a more active role in their future and help an evaluation of and a response to development needs.

- *Strategic growth*: major growth areas may occur adjacent to suburban areas, particularly on the urban fringe, giving rise to specific local opportunities.

In the following sub-sections, the range of potential opportunities related to each of these pressures is examined as the basis for selecting case studies and testing how far sustainable renewal may be achievable in these circumstances.

## Local investment

Public investment programmes may focus on suburban areas if they are experiencing a particular need (such as childcare). Private investment may be related to a niche opportunity, related to the specific nature of the suburb (such as a particular type of local workforce, or customer). But these pressures are normally found only in the extreme examples of deprivation or prosperity.

Generally the suburbs benefit from investment which is designed to serve the city as a whole. The most obvious example of this type of investment is that related to public transport improvements. There are several examples in the UK of recent initiatives – for instance, the Light Rapid Transit System designed to link the south London suburbs to Croydon. The issue is how far these types of improvements lead to opportunities for change in the suburban areas.

- Improved accessibility can change the image of an area making it more attractive as a residential area because of improved access to jobs, shopping and leisure facilities, and this may lead to increased investment by householders, with improvements to the housing stock.

- However, if the suburb is to benefit more generally from the improvements, there is normally a need for specific opportunities close to the new or improved public transport provision to enable development of additional facilities, housing types and mix of uses. Transport improvements may be considered a necessary element for change in some localities, but are unlikely to be sufficient to enable renewal.

The example of Portland, Oregon, is a relevant one in this context (City of Portland, 1993). The Light Rail project became the focus for planning land use development in the suburban areas in 1992, and the subject of a major investigation of opportunities around 'transit' stations. It was concluded that the main potential for sustainable renewal would be at the stations, with increased densities, mixed uses and higher riderships, but that it was vital to site the stations in relation to the land use opportunities (not select the station sites and then look for development opportunities).

A case study in the UK based on an existing public transport improvement would be useful in testing how far sustainable renewal can be pursued in this context.

## Rationalisation of provision

Rationalisation of facilities can take place both in the public and private sector, where organisational efficiency, desire to provide higher order services or commercial competition suggest that local branches or outlets are no longer an effective means of provision. In the public sector, changes in hospital provision and leisure facilities provide the most obvious examples, with many suburban areas suffering from the loss of local services.

In terms of private investment, the loss of local shopping is potentially one of the most damaging of changes in those areas where neighbourhood shops provide one of the few focuses of community life. Smaller suburban shopping centres may suffer from competition caused by:

- the spread of out of town facilities, often within the local catchment area, offering greater choice, competitive prices and easier parking

- the extension of opening hours in retail parks and superstores, to include 24-hour shopping facilities available seven days a week

- the priority given to supporting the vitality and viability of town centres, with investment in pedestrianisation, improved environment and range of specialist shopping.

There have been several studies examining the problems related to the rationalisation of retailing (LPAC, 1997). It may be necessary in some areas for a change in policy re-considering the size and role of these centres. There may be opportunities for the fringes of these local centres to provide new forms of residential accommodation, while elsewhere there may be possibilities for a new mix of employment, leisure and community uses.

A case study based on an area where there has been loss of retail would be useful in exploring how far alternative opportunities can be pursued to the benefit of the wider suburban mix.

## Local involvement

There is an increasing stress on social inclusion and community involvement as one of the main goals of sustainable development (Social Exclusion Unit at DETR, 1998). The aim is to enable local people to take a greater part in the planning and achievement of change in their area so that they increase their involvement in the wider community and its long-term success.

There are two current UK initiatives which are helping towards this aim.

- Devolution is being re-examined by some local authorities as they recognise the need to institute new forms of local governance that will make it more relevant to the community and enable it to serve local needs more accurately. There are examples of decentralised services delivered through interdisciplinary local teams in a locally based office. Elsewhere there are initiatives involving local organisations in considering potential solutions with access to a specified total budget. The thrust of government policy reflected in the recent Local Authority White Paper (1998) is very much to

encourage wider application of these principles.

- Local Agenda 21 has been enthusiastically adopted by most local authorities in the UK. The initiatives are intended to help people to identify specific environmental needs in the area, and then work together to bring about change, whether by improving an ecological area, introducing waste recycling, or local pedestrian or cycle routes, or influencing the design of new development. Until recently they have, however, been focused largely on 'green' issues rather than the full range of sustainable development factors.

The example of Vancouver is a useful one in this context (City of Vancouver, 1995). In considering a new city plan in the early 1990s the city authority decided to make public involvement central to the exercise. Using a wide variety of means including 'planning for real', a strategy was developed which centred largely on making Vancouver a 'city of neighbourhoods'. The local community identified a neighbourhood centre where they wanted to see change concentrated, and the range of uses they wanted, including local employment and urban spaces. A major change has been achieved in the neighbourhood delivery of municipal services.

A UK case study based in a city undertaking a major initiative in public involvement at the local level would help to test how far sustainable suburban renewal can be pursued in this context.

## Strategic growth

Large-scale growth can have a direct influence on suburban areas in close proximity. In some cases there are major accretions of a single large-scale use (a retail, leisure or business park), or a combination of these uses with major residential development.

These changes which separate the existing suburb from the countryside may have a number of positive and detrimental effects on the suburb.

- The new area of strategic growth may depend at least in its early stages on the provision of existing facilities in the neighbouring suburban area. This may have a beneficial effect in terms of increasing the viability of local facilities and utilising existing infrastructure, or it may cause problems by overloading existing facilities such as schools or health centres.

- The new area may provide new facilities which can be used by residents of the neighbouring suburb, enhancing the quality of life in that area. Increased leisure provision and employment are two of the most likely benefits.

- The new area may compete with existing facilities in the suburb and undermine them, leading to a deterioration in local services and community support. It may also bring unwelcome changes in transport patterns.

There is a considerable literature from America on the 'edge city' (Garreau, 1991; Leccese, 1992). Much of the focus of this work is on the way such developments can form one of a series of decentralised concentrations in the city region, and there is some debate as to whether such developments may have the potential if fully connected by public transport to help to increase the sustainability of cities (Breheny, 1992). The appropriate integration of such developments into the fabric of the existing suburbs would be an important test of sustainability.

A UK case study of the impact of a major urban-edge growth area on an adjoining suburb would be helpful in exploring how far existing suburbs may need to be helped to adapt to the change.

## Selection of case studies

In the light of the identification of these four types of 'drivers' of change which would be the focus of the case studies, the team then sought to identify an appropriate suburban location to test each of them. This was undertaken by a combination of desk analysis and consulation with a range of local authorities and other contacts, including the expert group which the subject of the semi-structured interviews referred to in Chapter 2 of this report.

A wide geographical distribution was sought, together with a good variety of housing tenure, a range of local market and development conditions, and a responsive local authority. Given the small size of the sample, we decided to focus on the suburbs of major cities, to provide a useful comparison, rather than examine suburbs in smaller urban centres. Aware both of the special market conditions that can apply in London, and the importance and scale of London's suburbs, we considered it essential that one of the studies should cover a London example.

The outcome of this intensive selection process, which was also tested with the Advisory Panel, was that we identified the following locations for the case studies:

- *Local investment*: North Tyneside, looking particularly at suburban evolution following the development of the Tyneside Metro.

- *Rationalisation of provision*: Redbridge in London, examining the impact of retail change on the suburban centres in the Borough.

- *Local involvement*: Northfield in Birmingham, studying the results of a major community engagement programme and its impact on attitudes.

- *Strategic growth*: North Bristol, assessing the evolution of these suburbs in the context of major development in the Cribbs Causeway area to the north.

## Approach to case studies

Each of the case study areas was examined using a common methodology and format, reflecting the issues and criteria identified from the earlier research and analysis.

The aim of this section of the research was to review the main drivers of change and to evaluate the extent to which such pressure can lead to the re-interpretation of an area in line with agreed principles of sustainable development.

Each case study required a review of the history and policy context relating to the key 'drivers' and a more general review of the suburban area as a whole. Detailed site visits were undertaken to provide the team with a clear understanding of the chosen area.

A focus group comprising senior officers from relevant departments of the local authority was assembled in each location to respond to the following key questions (a full list of questions is enclosed as Appendix 5).

- Why has change occurred?

- To what extent has it impacted upon the surrounding suburban area?

- How has the authority sought to actively manage this change in terms of the re-interpretation of the suburb as a more sustainable settlement?

- What are the lessons in this context for suburban renewal?

The team also approached estate agents and developers, as well as other local organisations such as housing associations and community groups which were active in the chosen area, to establish their perspective and to examine the opportunities and constraints which they perceived.

We should, however, emphasise that the resource limitations associated with this research meant that it was impossible to review a fully representative range of case studies. Instead the team has sought to select a number of locations which are acknowledged to have experienced pressures for change which we believe are common to other suburban locations across the UK.

# 7  Strategic growth and decentralisation: North Bristol

## Introduction

The northern suburbs of Bristol experienced rapid development over a period of approximately 40 years between 1930 and 1970. Since that time physical change has been slower, although significant social and economic shifts have occurred, notably the decline of major employment centres.

In contrast the area to the north of the City boundary, falling within a separate local government administration, has since 1980 been the major focus of new development for the whole Bristol conurbation. It has seen very substantial business and housing development and more recently the creation of large new retail and leisure facilities on a strategic scale. The momentum of this development is such that further expansion is likely.

The scale of this change is gradually shifting the relative location of the northern suburbs, insofar as they now sit between two strategic centres, Bristol city centre and the Cribbs Causeway/North Fringe complex. In part, though not entirely, this change is the result of deliberate planning by the local authorities and we will therefore focus on the manner in which the northern suburbs are adapting to change and the scope for a more sustainable programme.

## The pressure for change

The northern area of Bristol is defined as one of the four principal 'quarters' of the City by the City Council. The total population is 106,000. For the purposes of the case study, Avonmouth and Kingswestern have, however, been excluded, giving a residual population of 84,000. The area has an age profile similar to Bristol but with a slightly higher population of the retired. Socio-economic groupings correspond closely to the city average and two-thirds of housing was owner-occupied at

the 1997 Census, although this figure will have risen with continued purchases through 'right to buy' provisions. Significant municipal housing estates exist within the northern area, notably in Southmead, Longleaze and Henbury, but tenure, as indicated above, is now much more mixed.

## Economic development and employment

The area traditionally relied on Avonmouth, the aerospace plants at Filton to the north and to a lesser extent the city centre. In the last 15 years there has been a marked shift in employment. Approximately 40 per cent of residents work in the area, with a similar proportion now going to the city centre and most of the remainder working in the new strategic employment centres outside the City boundary to the north. Residents now travel further on average to work. Although the unemployment rate for the whole area is below the Bristol average, there are higher local concentrations which are seen as a significant problem.

## Housing stability

The northern area shows a considerable variety of house types and tenure, within the context of predominant owner occupation. The private rental sector is significant in the wards of Bishopston and Henleaze and there are indications that it is growing. The local authority housing stock is generally in good condition, reflecting major refurbishment programmes. The private housing stock is more mixed with some areas, with older properties and an ageing population, showing deterioration. This is particularly noticeable in the private rental sector.

Crime and security are significant issues in northern Bristol, although, in comparison with some other parts of the city, this area is not seen as justifying priority action. The exception is the Arnside area of Southmead which has been the subject of a specific programme involving the installation of CCTV.

## Transport changes

The shift in employment has led to changes in travel patterns. There used to be clear travel paths between living areas and traditional employers and these paths were well serviced by bus routes. Many people also cycled or walked. A comparison of the 1981 and 1991 Censuses shows a clear drop in the number of people in the area who travel to work on public transport. However, the fall in service does not necessarily reflect a fall in demand as there are still some employment generators in the area (for example Southmead Hospital and quite a lot of small businesses).

There are reasonably frequent bus services on radial routes, but much less so on orbital routes. Patterns of bus services have lacked co-ordination and review. Rail services are more encouraging – Filton Abbey Wood station opened in 1996 and there has been a consistently high customer demand and usage. However, the penetration of rail corridors into the area is limited and bus/rail integration is poor.

## Retailing revolution

Recent years have seen a significant number of retail developments on the edges of the northern suburbs area, mostly retail warehouses and a growth in discount supermarkets (such as Aldi and Lidl). However, there has recently been a major regional shopping centre development on the north fringe adding to existing retail at Cribbs Causeway. The effects of this development are as yet unknown, but may well be significant given the proximity to the northern area. The city centre has also been successful in attracting increased retail activity, increasing the pressure on the suburban centres.

In the face of these pressures, different suburban centres display different levels of success at maintaining vitality. Southmead estate has a new supermarket. Westbury Village is managing to hold its level of provision well. By contrast Gloucester Road (a long linear centre) in Bishopston has managed to hold on to a few specialist food shops, but at the same time has seen a significant decline in comparison shops (such as shoe or clothes shops), and a rising proportion of discount and charity shops with sharply increasing vacancy levels.

The number of 'corner' shops has also declined dramatically and so have small parades of shops. Conversion of failing/vacant retail outlets to leisure uses is a growing phenomenon. In some areas this shift is altering character (e.g. Whiteladies Road).

## Community and facilities

Overall the area has a relatively stable population. There are some ethnicity issues, but these are confined to small pockets of estates, in the northern suburbs. The local authority is currently running an English language programme with Asian women. Southmead and Lawrence Weston are areas with pockets of poverty and deprivation and are where much of the local authority's community work in North Bristol is focused.

There is a sense of local communities wanting to help themselves to improve their areas (especially in the pockets where there is a more elderly population) but they are in the main unable to identify the resources that they need. There is a strong sense of identity in each locality in the northern suburbs. Actual sense of community varies in strength. It tends to be stronger on definable estates and in 'natural community centres' such as shopping centres, and where there is a fairly stable population.

As well as the issue of shopping, there is considered to be a significant lack of community facilities, especially relating to young people and the elderly in several parts of the area. Local centres are seen as important, not merely for shopping, but also because they perform an identity role. When they decline, the 'morale' of the community can be significantly affected.

### Education and schools

With the advent of greater parental choice, there are problems of over-subscription in the more popular schools and, conversely, spare capacity at schools in the less popular areas. Another problem is parental dissatisfaction with (very linear) catchment areas. This has led to an increase in the number of people looking to the independent sector or schools outside the city and to a significant increase in the length of school journeys, with a drastic increase in trips by car and a marked decline in walking and cycling.

## Managing change

### Overall Council approach

There has recently been a re-organisation of the Council's structure. The City has been divided into four districts to enable implementation of an integrated service delivery in each, and the North forms one of these areas. There is a member-driver approach whereby key elected members are appointed to take the lead in each area and services are co-ordinated. The anticipated benefits of this are that people will be able to experience an integrated service (e.g. one-stop shops) but it is too early to judge the impact. It is also evident that the Council's officers are aware collectively of the many pressures for change and other difficulties identified.

### Development Plan and housing

Bristol's Urban Development Plan has just been adopted. Work began on it as long ago as 1992 and it is only designed to run until 2001. Current Development Plan policy tends to favour protection of the *status quo* – particularly in relation to green space, 'family' housing and a general presumption towards housing in character with existing buildings – primarily low density development.

Recent years have seen some losses of green space (most notably playing fields) to provide a superstore and two major housing developments. Change does happen, but generally is accepted only where significant/tangible change is already occurring. The prevailing local climate is one of suspicion towards development proposals and change.

The Development Plan has identified and earmarked some back-land for housing development. However, severe resistance from the localities is encountered when such proposals come forward. This has led to the curtailing of such initiatives. An example of a positive conversion policy is that which has supported a number of recent nursing home conversions. The Plan is reasonably adaptable towards conversions, and it is recognised that many elderly people in the area live alone in three/four bedroom houses, with little alternative accommodation locally available.

There is little in the current local plan which specifically encourages infill or general conversion, or other types of development which would result in a density increase. However, the local plan does not discourage higher density development and planners in Bristol are now beginning to re-consider this issue, and to recognise that policies may need to change.

It is possible that Council development and housing policy could adapt towards high quality small-scale intensification, provided change is gradual and incremental, but Members are likely to be wary. Much rests on the quality of the design solution, the transport dimension and the availability of community facilities.

### Transport policy

On public transport the local authority considers that its hands are tied by current legislation. There is only one major bus operator in the area but the authority has no control over routes other than through supported routes. The authority hopes the Transport White Paper will create the scope for change.

Figure 7.1 A good example of infill, Eastfield Terrace

Figure 7.2 New apartments, Gloucester Road

The network has only partially adapted to new developments. At the moment, for example, it is not possible to get to Cribbs Causeway by bus until 10.00 am. Operators are apparently considering putting on more buses – but to suit the needs of shoppers rather than staff. The result is that staff have no option but to travel to work by car. Very large free car parking areas are available in the new employment areas for both staff and customers.

One way in which the local authority has reacted to this has been to form a 'bus quality partnership' with the main operator. The partnership will be used mainly as a means of enhancing the existing services – for example, encouraging low-floor buses which are better for access. The partnership could also be used to suggest and promote new orbital routes. The authority sees it as important to improve orbital public transport so people can have better access not only to shops and services but also to other neighbourhoods.

The authority and the transport authorities are

also promoting a new light rapid travel (tram system) which will link the new strategic employment area in the north and the city centre. It will pass through part of the northern area with frequent stopping points. It is hoped to begin construction in 1999.

**Retail realism**

A clear response to the pressures for retail change and their impact on local communities is not very evident but some specific new development has been encouraged. For example, food stores can play a key anchor role, although the new supermarket at Southmead does not seem to have affected the local centre. Little action seems to have been taken in relation to the decline of areas such as Gloucester Road.

An example of sustainable community action to manage this retail problem exists in one part of northern Bristol, where local food producers have established themselves and there is now a successful local food market.

It appears that a number of retail frontages with a limited retail future in the northern suburbs could merit consideration for 'living over the shop' schemes, and perhaps conversion of ground floor premises from retail to residential, or even wholesale re-development. The authority previously operated a small LOTS (Living Over The Shop) programme but this has resulted in few actual conversions.

The authority is cautious of converting too many retail premises to residential as they want to protect the existing retail hierarchy and in cases of defined retail frontages this would be a departure from the local plan. It is also wary of environmental/design barriers – for example quality of life for people living in retail areas that are situated on linear routes would not be particularly high because of high levels of traffic. But the authority does acknowledge the need for change.

**Community potential**

There are some interesting examples of community action. These include two credit unions in the northern suburbs; a Single Regeneration Budget (SRB) funded green networks project; a city farm; a development trust and a neighbourhood trust. Overall, there is much community activity, but a significant shortage of resources. There is also some Local Agenda 21 activity, which provides good examples of effective community activity.

A team of community development workers based in Southmead covers the district, supporting community-led projects in all areas.

The other main problem in harnessing community potential is a lack of support staff. Partnership 'building' takes much time and patience, requiring a considerable injection of public resources, in order to restore staff cuts and support a greater voluntary sector contribution.

A large part of Bristol's northern suburbs, however, currently fall below thresholds for government grant aid.

**Community planning**

The local authority has in the past considered the production of 'neighbourhood statements' as spin-offs to local plans. However, this approach was expensive in staff time. Ideally communities would prefer to have their 'own' figurehead with whom they can identify. There is resistance to such a figurehead being from the voluntary or private sector as communities see provision of a community worker as the local authority's responsibility.

'Planning for real' has worked well in some places. There is sometimes a tendency for these exercises to be seen as 'parachuting' in and then back out of an area. But in Bristol the community development workers have helped to maintain the momentum afterwards, and Local Agenda 21 and other partnerships are beginning to change the 'culture'.

The Leader of the Council encourages active local democracy and community engagement. This process is about more than just money. More important is the need to develop ways to help people become more aware of resources available, maximise their access to those resources and become more involved in the decision-making process.

### Local politics

Local politicians understandably tend to focus on the specific and short term as a priority, reflecting the flow of the current electorate's line of thinking. Wider strategic and longer-term issues do not command the same attention, even though their impact may be profound over time. At the moment that means politicians are wary of policies which would result in a noticeable shift in the *status quo*. The local community focus is on reacting to specific development proposals and threats to local amenities such as schools.

## Conclusions

### Integrated strategic planning

It would be wrong to characterise the area as exhibiting a lack of strategic planning. The rapid development of the very substantial, road-based, new development area to the north of Bristol has occurred at a time when a full development planning process has been operational. Yet we are left with the strong impression that the implications of the scale of change for Bristol's northern suburbs have, until recently, not been closely monitored or sufficiently coherently addressed. The new developments rely very heavily on car access and little has been done to adapt other transport with the partial exception of heavy rail. Their implications for already vulnerable local retail facilities, which in turn offer support to other valued community facilities, are largely unknown and an overall policy response is not evident. Adaptations to the local housing and jobs market to reflect the virtual emergence of a new 'city centre' to the north of the area have not been identified or

encouraged. A timescale of six years to produce a development plan which then has an effective life of only four years must be of concern. Bristol's new status as a unitary authority, coupled with the greater powers for transport co-ordination emerging from the Transport White Paper, will therefore need to be used as positive levers and set in a positive context of more effective co-operation with neighbouring authorities.

### Positive policies and plans

It is evident that the Council officers and most of the other groups interviewed are well aware of a range of potential pressures and problems. There are also examples of positive responses, for example, new retail and housing developments, housing conversion schemes for the elderly, the new railway station and community initiatives such as the Agenda 21 network. Many development decisions, however, seem to have been specific and reactive rather than reflecting a corporate and positive response. Priorities understandably have been focused elsewhere in the city or on a few specific municipal estates. There has been little political encouragement to take a broader or long-term view. In resource terms, much of the area does not qualify for grants or other special assistance. The establishment of the new area structure with its emphasis on coalition is, however, a most encouraging initiative which has the potential to overcome many of the problems. Coupled with the review of development plans which will shortly be required, it provides an opportunity to take a much more positive stance.

### Transport investment

The transport dimension is very important to both the present and future of North Bristol and yet represents something of a 'curate's egg'! On the one hand there has been very substantial investment in road activities. On the other there has been relatively little investment in or adaptation to the other modes. The lack of evolution of the bus

**Figure 7.3 Time for change? Prefabs, Southmead**

**Figure 7.4 Time for change? Prefabs, Horsefield**

network is astonishing but partly reflects the lack of coherent national and regional transport policy over the last decades. Encouragingly the Council is clearly well seized of this issue and with better government support could now begin to at least *recreate* the more sustainable transport choices that formerly existed.

**Community support and area management**

The strength of local community identity, the existence of community networks, the awareness of local authority officers and the example of a number of community initiatives all provide a positive foundation for the development of 'community plans' in North Bristol which could assess both community needs and development potential in an integrated manner. There is, however, a considerable degree of wariness and suspicion to be overcome. The first and crucial step is to build community involvement and confidence, before setting out options for change. This will require the mobilisation of all local authority and other resources in the area, following the principles of the Local Government Association's *New*

*Commitments Programme.* It will also mean encouraging the voluntary sector to play a greater part.

In this context the scope for developing a gradual and limited process of renewal and re-development should be explored, not as a means of 'imposing' housing numbers, but as a way of responding to local needs.

The problem of declining community facilities, for example, might be met by the re-development of existing sites, with a combination of sheltered housing and purpose-built new facilities, using the Private Finance Initiative (*PPP*). New leisure facilities such as tennis centres might be provided in a similar manner. The adaptation of declining local centres with a new mix of housing and other uses might be similarly encouraged. Successful conversion and infill housing schemes built in the area and elsewhere could be identified so that their positive lessons could be applied. The adaptation of local bus services, and facilities for cycling and walking could be set by community debate and

**Figure 7.5  Scope for a small re-development?**

**Figure 7.6  Longer-term potential? TA Centre, North Bristol**

linked closely to these changing patterns of activity and land use.

Such a process would reflect local political concerns and priorities yet set them in a wider and longer-term context. It would not seek to achieve drastic change in the short term, but over time it could allow a significant degree of housing change and adaptation, in a sustainable development context.

**Pilots**

It is evident that both the local authority officers and others in the area increasingly see the need for change and for a new approach. The City Council's recent initiatives reflect a similar awareness, but it is difficult to build confidence and demonstrate the scope for change without examples. In discussions it became evident that there is a need for a small number of 'pilot' initiatives to be taken forward in North Bristol to show what might be more widely

**Figure 7.7  Retail decay, Gloucester Road**

**Figure 7.8  Vacant shop and flats, Southmead**

**Figure 7.9 Ageing community facilities, Bishopston and Eastfield Lane**

**Figure 7.10 Scope for private capital for leisure facilities? Horsefield**

achieved. The officers would like to support such an approach but at present they are too busy with day to day duties. Initiatives that combined a fresh look at design and development opportunities, with a very strong community focus, using private finance, would make sense. They might focus on a new community leisure centre, the refurbishment and re-development of a shopping area, or the re-development of a small cluster of existing houses overlooking an open space to create apartments. We have illustrated some possible examples, but more detailed analysis would be needed.

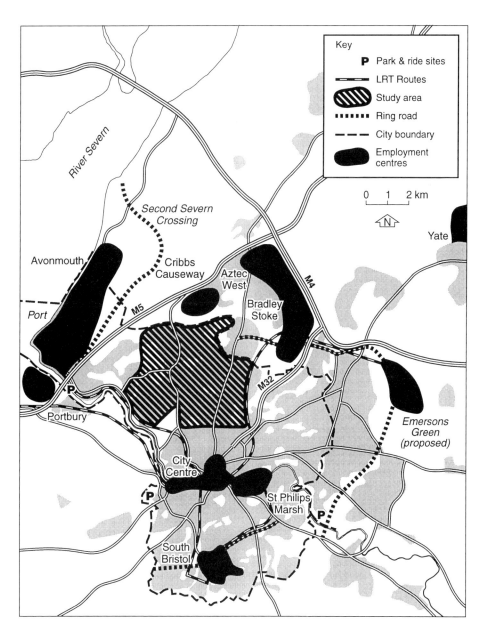

**Figure 7.11  North Bristol Study Area**

# 8 Re-inventing retail: The Redbridge experience

## Introduction

The retail economy across the London Borough of Redbridge reflects, to a degree, the recent pattern of growth and decline in suburban retailing across the UK. While some local centres are experiencing significant growth through increased private investment, other centres are becoming problematic in terms of environmental decline, a decreasing range of shops and services, and increasing vacancies.

Our research has indicated that the loss of local retailing in suburban areas is likely to undermine sustainable development goals. As the range of local services is reduced, the need to travel further is increased, resulting in greater car dependency, increased road traffic and pollution, and increased social isolation for people without access to private transport.

## The pressure for change

### Economic dependence on London

Ilford is the main centre for retail and commerce in Redbridge, a borough situated to the north-east of central London. The borough can be principally defined as residential, with a number of suburban centres comprising a spread of nineteenth and twentieth century suburban semis and terraces. Proximity to London, the City and the Docklands has led to an economic reliance on the services and employment of central London, although there are a number of industrial estates catering for small- and medium-sized businesses across the borough. There are only two large private sector employers in Ilford: British Aerospace (formerly Siemens) and Britannia Music. The London Borough of Redbridge, and Redbridge and Waltham Forest Health Authority also provide a substantial amount of employment in the public sector.

### Growth of out of town retail

Most major multiples are represented in Ilford and many quality comparison goods shops can be found. In terms of retailing, Ilford is a successful town centre, with low vacancies and considerable rate of expansion. Since the mid-1980s, the centre has benefited from extensive public investment, including the pedestrianisation of the High Road and the development of The Exchange shopping centre, opened in 1991, which provided additional space for some 70 new retail businesses. More recently, Marks & Spencer and Next have demonstrated their commitment to the town centre by investing in store expansion. Waterstone's, the booksellers, has recently moved into Ilford.

The Council is keen for Ilford to consolidate and strengthen its retailing position in view of its proximity to the out of town leisure and retail development at Lakeside Thurrock and the new, even larger regional centre currently under construction at Bluewater Park in Dartford. Ilford is well within the catchment for both these centres and it is almost certain that increased pressure from Bluewater Park will threaten the local retail economy. The new A13, due for completion in 1999, will add to the threat posed by Lakeside and Bluewater Park by improving accessibility to their out of town facilities.

Ilford is reliant on comparison goods retailing and cannot compete with the leisure facilities offered at Lakeside and, potentially, at Bluewater Park. Evening and leisure uses in Ilford are limited to a small theatre, a few pubs on Cranbrook Road and a few night clubs at the eastern end of the High Road. The paucity of sports, leisure and other facilities for youth is a matter of concern for a number of community groups. The Council has responded to these concerns and is currently encouraging a structural expansion of leisure activity with plans to develop a new cinema and leisure complex close to the site of the existing Town Hall.

There is little in terms of food retailing in Ilford town centre, with the exception of an edge of centre Sainsbury's and the town centre Marks & Spencer store. The vibrant cluster of Asian stores along Ilford Lane to the south-west complements the town centre by supplying a range of cheap and bulk-buy groceries catering specifically for the local Asian and Afro-Caribbean communities.

**Car dependency**

The borough is relatively well served by public transport, with underground and mainline stations providing links to both London and the Essex coast. Despite this, statistics show evidence of high car ownership and increasing car dependency across the borough (London Borough of Redbridge, Residents' Survey, 1998). According to local estate agents, home owners seek *both* access to good public transport *and* good home parking facilities – it is not unusual to find three or four car households in the area. While many local residents are not dependent on their cars for access to employment, local community groups and estate agents claim that car ownership is seen as essential for access to retail and leisure facilities for most social groups. The bus network is mainly used by elderly members of the local population.

The negative impact of this dependency on private transport is increased traffic congestion. This has been identified as *the* key concern of local residents across Redbridge in a recent survey (London Borough of Redbridge, Residents' Survey, 1998).

**Changes in the local centres**

The absence of high quality leisure facilities and food retailers in Ilford town centre has, in part, enabled surrounding suburban centres to survive, with complementary services available in smaller suburban centres across the borough. For example,

cinemas are presently located at South Woodford and Gants Hill; the Borough's main swimming pool and leisure centre is situated in Barkingside; and major food retailers have recently invested in stores in Barkingside and South Woodford – where there currently appears to be a battle between the major supermarket chains for maximum presence.

However, while Barkingside, South Woodford and Wanstead have seen economic growth in recent years, particularly linked to retail investment, other smaller shopping centres at Gants Hill, Seven Kings and Goodmayes have an aura of decline, with high vacancy levels and a poor retail environment.

*South Woodford* and *Wanstead* are the most affluent suburban centres in Redbridge, both located at the western edge of the borough with a prosperous population and catchment of larger, owner-occupied, semi-detached and detached Victorian and Edwardian houses and relatively attractive town centres. South Woodford boasts an ABC cinema and a Sainsbury's supermarket in addition to a new Waitrose currently being built. Wanstead is perceived as a 'village' centre and as such has an attractive small-scale retail environment with a range of small, often expensive boutiques and independent retailers.

*Barkingside* is a successful centre to the north of the borough. It has thrived despite its relatively unattractive linear, inter-war retail environment stretching from the Fulwell Cross roundabout to the junction of Tanners Lane to the south. Although there is a relatively high number of low-budget retailers and charity shops, the centre benefits from a number of factors including a leisure centre and library, investment in a major Tesco superstore just south of the high street, and the fortunate fact that a number of buses end their routes in Barkingside bringing elderly and carless shoppers from estates in Hainault and Woodford. The arrival of the Tesco superstore, in addition to the existing Sainsbury's store, has secured Barkingside's status as a significant secondary retail centre by offering high

**Figure 8.1 An unfriendly pedestrian environment and a threatened cinema, Gants Hill**

quality food retailing not available in Ilford, attracting customers not only from Redbridge but from more affluent parts of Essex to the north.

*Gants Hill, Seven Kings* and *Goodmayes* have been identified as the suburban centres in Redbridge suffering most from decline and under-investment. *Gants Hill* is a small suburban centre situated at a roundabout which provides a focal point for five roads including the A12, A123 and the A1400 trunk roads. The centre is approximately an equal distance from larger retail centres at Barkingside, South Woodford and Ilford. It is a major transport focus with the Central line station located underground at the centre of the roundabout, linked to a substantial bus network by a web of subways. Three of the roads approaching the Gants Hill junction are dual carriageways which are notoriously difficult for pedestrians to cross at street level. Vehicular traffic seems to have priority over pedestrian movement, resulting in a largely unattractive, highly congested and polluted environment.

Although its proximity to a large residential catchment and excellent accessibility should in theory seem attractive to retailers, the area has suffered from serious decline and lack of investment for some years. The closure of the multi-storey car park situated just to the south of

the centre is likely to have contributed to its decline. The majority of retail units are situated along Cranbrook Road, the only single carriageway road passing across the roundabout from north to the south. Only specialist retailing has survived, with kosher food shops catering for the large local Jewish community. Of the other units, some are vacant, while some have converted to restaurants or takeaways or night clubs. An old-style Odeon cinema is situated just off the roundabout on Perth Road.

It is widely thought that the poor pedestrian environment, lack of adequate parking facilities and competition from neighbouring centres have contributed to the current decline of the centre.

The proximity of *Seven Kings* to Ilford town centre has contributed towards the decline in retailing in the area. The centre is poorly served by public transport and its unattractive linear design is not welcoming. The dominance of second-hand car dealerships, particularly to the east of the centre, has had a negative impact on general retailing at this end of town and there is a great concentration of vacancy here. Excluding car dealerships, only 40 per cent of units are currently in retail use, and these are predominantly small, independent food retailers and newsagents. The eastern section of the High Street is dominated by a large Sainsbury's

Figure 8.2 A transport node with potential?

Homebase store, a large public house, a petrol filling station and a disused bus garage (which now has permission for retail development). At the time of the borough-wide 'health check' in 1994, the Council was struggling to preserve retail use in the High Street and has refused several applications for change of use to A2 or A3.

*Goodmayes* is situated further to the east of Ilford. Its centre is somewhat disjointed, comprising a retail park along the High Road (with a large Tesco superstore), a stretch of mixed retailing along Goodmayes Road and a range of independent convenience stores at the junction of Green Lane. The main shopping facilities are located at the fringe of the centre – at the retail park and at the junction of Green Lane. The centre suffers from a poor pedestrian environment, buildings in a poor condition, and general noise and pollution problems caused by traffic intrusion. The Tesco store on the High Road is Goodmayes' major anchor store, although it is unlikely that its presence has contributed much to the overall quality of the centre. There is a fairly high turnover of retail units and a high number of applications for change of use from retail to A2 or A3 uses. At the time of the borough-wide 'health check' in 1994, the Council had allowed a number of takeaways and

cafes in secondary streets and change of use to A2 in the prime shopping area.

**Housing**
The borough has a low proportion of council housing (and political resistance to an increase from certain groups) and a significant distinction of character between the north and south of the borough. In the north (beyond the A12) the housing stock is predominantly owner-occupied and mostly in good condition. In the south of the borough the housing is generally older, mostly late nineteenth century and early twentieth century. This part of the borough has traditionally supplied cheaper housing and, as such, has attracted lower income households, including a large number of immigrants. While much of the housing stock is owner-occupied and in good condition, there is an overall perception that housing condition in the area is poorer and in some areas actually shows marked signs of decline. There has been a significant growth in the private rental sector and conversions in this area, and some of this property's condition is now giving rise to real concern. There are fluid and fragmented ownership patterns in the southern part of the borough, reflecting in part the transient population of the private rental sector.

**Figure 8.3 A high number of vacant units**

According to local estate agents, the more sought after parts of the borough are in Wanstead and Woodford, where houses are larger and the streets more leafy. However, parts of Gants Hill – namely the Woods Estate and the Garden City – are also considered to be very desirable. The price of property in these parts of Gants Hill reflects current demand with a typical four-bedroom house valued from £150K in the Woods Estate to £250K in the Garden City. This contrasts significantly with the value of similar properties in Barkingside, Hainault or South Ilford where a four-bedroom house would be valued below £100K.

The quality of local retailing and leisure facilities is not necessarily a key factor determining the decisions of home buyers. Estate agents have identified other factors influencing home buying, including: access to public transport (for links to the City), car parking facilities and nearby good schools. The good educational facilities and excellent range of schools in Redbridge attract many families from the inner city boroughs. Secondary schools in Redbridge have an excellent reputation. Moreover, there are two grammar schools plus specialist secondary schools, one catering for the Jewish community which attracts Jewish families from across London.

Crime, or rather the perception of crime, is a major issue throughout the borough, although the actual incidence of crime is not high. A 'safe community partnership' has been established to try to provide resonance and strengthen community feeling. Local businesses and community representatives in the Ilford Lane area have heralded the initiative as a success in terms of the development of partnerships between the local ethnic population, the local authority and the police.

## Managing change

The Council officers are aware of the difficulties facing Gants Hill, Seven Kings and Goodmayes, and are particularly concerned about the future of Gants Hill. To date, however, attention in terms of policy and investment appears to have been focused on Ilford town centre, partially in order to strengthen the economic base of the borough in the face of competition from out of town retail centres. Consequently, until recently, there has been little acknowledgement of the problems facing the secondary centres. Although the current Urban Development Plan (UDP) and the Economic Development Plan recognise these issues, the changes that have taken place to date, in terms of growth and decline across the borough, seem to have been determined largely by market forces.

Likewise, certain factors having a major impact on changes in the suburban centres are perceived to be external to Council influence. For example, the deteriorating environment has been, at least in part, attributed to the influx of cars passing through the borough from Essex to central London. While public transport links are good across the borough, links to new employment centres such as Greenwich and the Docklands are perceived as inadequate. The Jubilee line extension may go part way to improving linkages and the Council is currently reviewing plans to introduce a public transport link between Gants Hill and Barking which will improve accessibility to the Docklands.

Development is constrained by the physically compact nature of settlement in the borough. Residential and commercial development sit side by side across the borough with little vacant brownfield land available for new development. Much of the borough brushes against Green Belt land which restricts development further.

The Council has limited capacity to address the need for improved suburban housing, although it has adopted an 'empty property strategy', and has initiated a 'living over the shop' programme. Change of use to residential is also encouraged where appropriate. However, any proposed increase in housing density and proposals for new development are constrained by elected members' concerns about over-development. Rather than allow new development on infill sites, members have recently secured some potential housing sites as nature reserves. An added constraint is that parking standards for new development remain high.

Where re-development is most needed, in the south of the borough, mixed ownership patterns and the relatively small-scale properties prohibit wholesale change, but significant incremental

change is occurring through, for example, conversions. Parking standards for conversion schemes have often been relaxed and an effective increase in densities is accepted. Conversions are thus creating a considerable number of housing gains per annum. Given the condition of some of the stock, some large-scale re-development would make increasing sense and help address concerns about a loss of character.

Employment patterns give limited scope for change in reducing travel. There is little basis for a substantial increase in employment within the borough and new employment opportunities developing to the south of the Borough are likely to increase rather then reduce commuting flows. There is, however, scope for re-thinking traffic patterns, to reduce the impact of car traffic on much of the borough and to remodel bus services to review their present routes. Little of this has been attempted in recent years in the absence of a strategic transport authority.

The lack of a strategic transport authority and a general lack of financial resources were identified by officers as the main constraints on long-term planning. The short elective cycle of the local councillors results in short-term projects with maximum impact being prioritised. Engagement with the local community – particularly minority groups – has been scarce. Now the decline in suburban centres is becoming increasingly apparent, the Council is starting to react and incremental policy changes are emerging. Resources to encourage and support developmental change and regular 'health checks' are scarce and 'not a priority'. There are few funds at any level of government to commit to areas like suburban Redbridge which are relatively low on the index of social deprivation, and the trend of government policy seems likely to make programmes such as SRB (Single Regeneration Budget) ever more focused.

Policy changes which have taken place in the borough in response to the need for increased sustainable development in suburban areas, include steps taken to:

- convert larger residential homes for care homes, day nurseries and independent schools

- reduce parking requirements for residential conversions

- convert houses to multi-occupancy flats or studios

- accept, at least in principle, the need for a marked increase in residential densities as suggested in the recent Llewelyn-Davies (1998) study for LPAC

- convert offices to residential use in the Gants Hill area

- promote leisure and evening activities in Gants Hill.

There are opportunities for further sustainable, high density, residential or mixed use development initiatives in the borough. For instance in Ilford town centre the BT tower has been identified for possible conversion to housing and in Gants Hill some institutional landowners have been identified

and there is potential for a significant re-development initiative. The location of Gants Hill, being so close to transport nodes, renders it suitable for residential development for young or single member households and this would sit well with the increased range of evening uses now being encouraged in the area, but only if the centre's high degree of transport accessibility becomes seen as an opportunity rather than a problem. The other declining centres are very concentrated physically and re-development options appear limited.

In the south of the borough the scope for new conversions and selective smaller-scale re-development also needs to expand, to seek to consolidate the environmental shift of policy in recent years. The community dimension would, however, need very careful attention, given a number of sensitivities.

## Conclusions

### Positive policies and plans

To date, the majority of policy decisions concerning suburban areas have been taken as a *reaction* to issues arising across the borough rather than as *pro-active* measures to halt or indeed reverse decline. Priorities have been focused elsewhere, although

**Figure 8.4 Residential conversion to a children's nursery, Redbridge**

the borough development plan has given a broad overall framework. As a result, policy decisions towards issues relating to change of use or house conversions or parking standards have lacked cohesion. There is a clear need, then, for the Council to set out a detailed vision and strategic framework to guide the future of the suburban centres, to address the issue of decline head on. In the case of Gants Hill, for example, the piecemeal approach to change, which has comprised to date encouraging change of use to leisure (A3), has not led to any significant improvement in appearance and perception of the centre. A more radical approach to renewal could be achieved with a more strategic approach to addressing the problems faced by small suburban centres backed up by focused local programmes for each centre. *Some design ideas for a radical restructuring of the Gants Hill area are set out in Figure 8.8.*

### Design projects

Council officers expressed concern regarding the lack of appropriate and inspirational 'best practice' examples of the regeneration of suburban centres.

**Figure 8.5 Residential conversion to a residential care home, Redbridge**

**Figure 8.6 Scope for people-friendly improvement, Gants Hill (see Figure 8.8)**

While there is wide acknowledgement of the problems of decline in suburban centres amongst the officers, there appears to be little consensus on an approach to addressing the main issues. It was suggested that a pilot project to demonstrate what could be achieved in a 'typical' suburban centre – through investment, community involvement or Council strategy – would provide a useful tool for local authorities in similar predicaments to draw on.

### Strategic planning and transport authority

Transport impact and disturbance as well as access to public transport is a major issue of concern in Redbridge, but the problem is principally metropolitan rather than confined to the borough boundaries. The borough's location between East Anglia/Essex and central London has resulted in it becoming a virtual 'thoroughfare' for commuting traffic. Likewise, public transport does not serve the whole borough adequately and has not adapted to changing patterns of employment. Links to the Docklands and Greenwich, for example, are poor and the entire public transport network seems to be under-used for evening and leisure purposes. The new Greater London Authority therefore will have a critical role and hopefully the potential to resolve transportation issues across borough boundaries. Until this is done, the scope for more sustainable transport and land use patterns in the borough will be relatively limited.

### Staff resources

Although there was recognition of the scope for change, there was also concern amongst officers about a lack of staff time to undertake work on the issues affecting the suburban centres, especially in terms of engaging and involving the local community. Available staff time was currently focused on other priorities; this issue would need to be addressed.

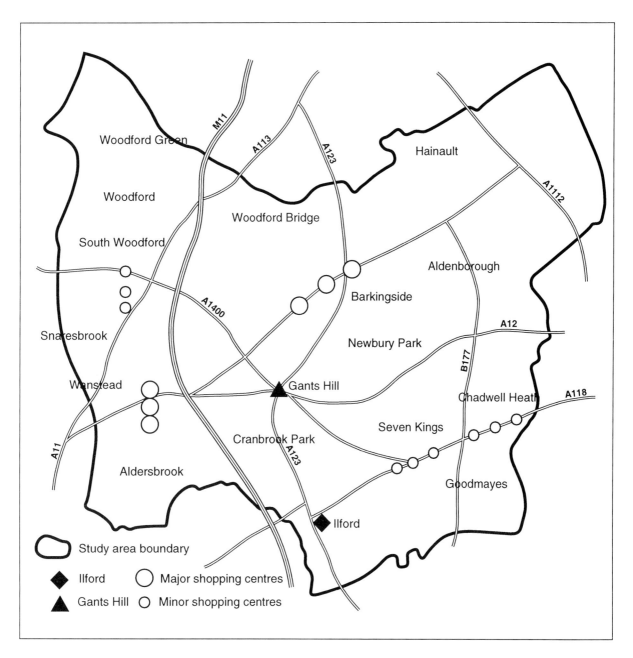

**Figure 8.7 London Borough of Redbridge Study Area**

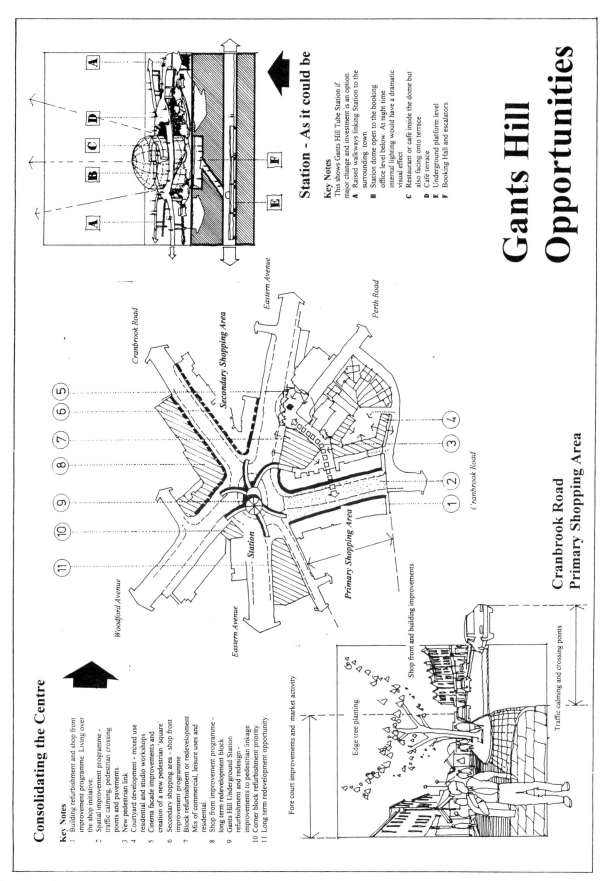

## Consolidating the Centre

**Key Notes**

1  Building refurbishment and shop front improvement programme. Living over the shop initiative.
2  Spatial improvement programme - traffic calming, pedestrian crossing points and pavements.
3  New pedestrian link.
4  Courtyard development - mixed use residential and studio workshops.
5  Cinema facade improvements and creation of a new pedestrian 'square'
6  Secondary shopping area - shop front improvement programme.
7  Block refurbishment or redevelopment Mix of commercial, leisure uses and residential.
8  Shop front improvement programme - long term redevelopment block.
9  Gants Hill Underground Station refurbishment and redesign - improvements to pedestrian linkage.
10  Corner block refurbishment priority.
11  Long term redevelopment opportunity.

### Station - As it could be

**Key Notes**

This shows Gants Hill Tube Station if major change and investment is an option.

A  Raised walkways linking Station to the surrounding town.
B  Station dome open to the booking office level below. At night time internal lighting would have a dramatic visual effect.
C  Restaurant or café inside the dome but also facing onto terrace.
D  Café terrace.
E  Underground platform level.
F  Booking Hall and escalators.

# Gants Hill Opportunities

**Cranbrook Road Primary Shopping Area**

Fore court improvements and market activity.

Edge tree planting.

Shop front and building improvements.

Traffic calming and crossing points

**Figure 8.8  Gants Hill proposals**

48

# 9  Local investment: North Tyneside

## Introduction

Public transport is a crucial element for a sustainable renewal strategy. It helps to reduce levels of energy consumption and car pollution, and increase accessibility for different uses and groups of people, providing the foundation for more balanced communities. Usually suburbs are particularly short of public transport and this affects their functional and social mix. However, a pro-active public transport strategy, although desirable in itself, is very expensive and may not directly promote other processes of social, economic and physical regeneration.

The selected case of Willington Quay/Howdon, in North Tyneside, fits in the context of our research in terms of the positive combination of two drivers for change:

- impact of public transportation (Tyne and Wear Metro)

- strategically located land becoming available for development.

## The pressure for change

North Tyneside is one of the five unitary authorities in the former County of Tyne and Wear, located north-east of Newcastle. It has a population of around 190,000 (1991 Census), as a result of a 9 per cent drop over the preceding 20 years.

The whole area is generally 'suburban' in terms of housing types and appearance. However, it has always contained a high proportion of employment sites, especially along the river and the old north-south mineral railway. Consequently the area has in the past had a certain degree of self-containment, based on heavy industry, now being replaced by light industry and business development. According to the 1991 Census, 25,000 people commute to Newcastle, 37,000 stay in the area and 22,000 come to the area from outside.

The residential areas are usually of the medium density, suburban type. Housing land uses are mixed with employment and green areas. There is no one clear centre but a series of local centres (such as Killingworth, North Shields and Wallsend). The existence of the Metro and the older suburbs in the eastern part of North Tyneside have helped to balance the polarisation effect of Newcastle. The level of car ownership is comparatively low.

The Tyne and Wear Metro, running in a circuit throughout the whole area (Fig. 9.3), uses the infrastructure of an earlier suburban railway line. The Electric Service serving the sea coast villages was set up in 1908. Following this, it went through a period of decline from the 1960s.

Since 1969 a major land use/transportation strategy has been set in place to regenerate and improve the original electrified system, creating a light metro line to serve the whole metropolitan area. This strategy was aimed at creating an integrated transport system with re-routed buses feeding into the Metro stations. As much as possible buses were seen as a means to commute to the stations, rather than directly into town, in order to avoid street congestion.

The Metro is the key element of what is considered a very successful and popular public transport integrated system. Since its introduction, the number of journeys by public transport in Tyne and Wear has increased significantly, while they have declined nationally. In 1984/85, the first year of full operation, passenger boardings peaked at 61.1 million. In the following years patronage declined, mainly because of the reduction of buses feeding into the Metro, as a result of deregulation. Journeys to work account for around 42 per cent of Metro journeys (1988 data). The second most popular reason for using the Metro is shopping and this explains why Saturday is the peak day.

The line was originally designed to serve the developing suburbs, especially along the coast. However, many other estates have been developed in North Tyneside since then, taking advantage of the transport connections. The Metro has determined the way the area works but has not revolutionised it. In general, research (TRL, 1993) shows that changes in the proximity to the Metro appeared to have had only a very localised effect on the housing market, with a 2 per cent enhancement in property values around stations.

Since the mid-1980s, the implementation of the transport strategy has meant that some new stations have been opened or moved. Stations such as Palmersville and Hadrians Road have been opened along the existing line. The station of Shiremoor has been moved in order to better serve the residential area, and for technical, railway-related reasons, and this has produced a significant change in property values.

The focus of the analysis in the next section is on the change promoted by a site becoming available for development in the *Willington Quay* area, adjacent to Howdon Metro station and separated from the area of *Howdon* only by the railway line (Fig. 9.2). Here we will look at the characteristics of the wider area, north and south of the site, and other local regeneration strategies.

Willington Quay is located in the southern part of North Tyneside, enclosed between the Metro line and the river. The southern part of the area adjacent to the river accommodates mainly industrial uses. Generally, the whole area south of the Metro line is used for industrial purposes. The presence of a residential area of around 1,500 people south of the Metro is an exception to the general rule that housing in this area was seen as non-desirable, because of isolation in a non-appropriate environment.

Willington Quay was originally built as a suburb related to the heavy industries along the river. Industrial land and the rail line have always physically separated it from the northern residential part of Howdon. Historically it enjoyed a balance of population and local employment opportunities. Following the decline of the

industrial activities in the area, this is no longer the case. It is characterised by a variety of semi-detached and terraced housing of different periods ranging from about 1900 to the present, mostly privately owned or rented (Fig. 9.1). The area is small but has a well integrated structure but with very few non-residential uses. The whole area is short of commercial premises and depends on Newcastle, Wallsend or North Shields for shopping.

Howdon, to the north of the Metro line, has a population of 9,000. The area has mainly been built in the post-war period. It is mainly residential, with 52 per cent privately owned or rented and 48 per cent Council owned. Some shopping is situated along the A193 crossing west-east and in a small cluster at the centre of the area. There are no substantial facilities in the area. A study by University of Newcastle on health conditions in the Northern Region identified this as one of the worst areas of the country in terms of health indicators. The property market is also not doing well, with people abandoning private properties in the western part of the ward.

In terms of community, the two areas are clearly differentiated, but the population of Howdon has shown an attachment for the newly created green area in the eastern part of Willington Quay, which is looked after by a local residents' association. The Metro station and the few shops and facilities are the points of physical contact between the two communities.

Willington Quay has been neglected by the urban regeneration strategies undertaken in the area. The south part of North Tyneside along the river was part of the Tyne and Wear Development Corporation. However, the UDC focused most of its efforts on flagship schemes such as the Royal Quays. Interestingly, this approach was already used in the Willington Quay Local Plan some 20 years ago. However, despite the opportunity of the site becoming available for development, the plan did not deliver. It would be interesting to investigate the reasons for this. It may be that this

Figure 9.1 Typical mix of housing in Willington Quay and Howden, North Tyneside

was prevented by the presence of other opportunities around – greenfield and Tyne and Wear Development Corporation schemes – which were easier to realise and by the lack of effective comprehensive funding regimes. Probably, the situation on both aspects is now different.

## Managing change

In the mid-1980s the Willington Quay/Howdon area was suffering from de-industrialisation with hardly any investment. In the late 1970s the area between Rosehill Road and Howdon Lane became available for development (Fig. 9.2). The Council bought half of the site in 1979 from Howdon Gas Works. *'Derelict Land Grant'* money was used to undertake decontamination of the site.

From the beginning, the Council saw the development of this site as an opportunity to regenerate the whole area, with a mixed-use development which would allow for the provision of housing and local facilities. The focus has been on the role played by this area to create a link between the two parts north and south of the Metro line, and a centre for the overall community, with shopping and public facilities. Housing development was considered as a way to re-connect the two parts of the urban structure, offer alternative types of housing to the local population and provide some planning benefits for local facilities such as the Stephenson Memorial First School. Industrial activities remain in many of the sites surrounding Willington Quay and proposals include some employment uses in the land to be developed.

Five developers were approached. Only Bellway responded positively, feeling they could develop the area following the Council indications, with the help of English Partnerships. In the area there is a demand for two–four bedroom new houses from local people who want to remain in the area, within their communities. Similar new developments have recently taken place in areas such as Wallsend.

The Council guidelines presented in the land disposal documents produced in April 1997 indicate that the aim was to create more than an inward-looking residential estate. The Council was in principle in favour of selling the land but with a certain number of conditions, among which were the following:

- Bellway securing English Partnerships funding

- Bellway securing an agreement with Guinness Trust for the purchase of 100 dwellings

- Bellway and Guinness Trust giving priority to sell and rent dwellings to people nominated by the Council

- Bellway paying to the Council, in addition, not less than 25 per cent of any average sale price of the housing units over and above the base unit price assessed by English Partnership

- Bellway constructing a replacement school on the site of the Stephenson Memorial First School.

A first draft plan was presented by Bellway satisfying most on the Council's expectations by providing close to the Metro Station a neighbourhood centre, commerce, a community centre and other public facilities. Subsequently, a large-scale commercial element suggested for the site via a commercial agent modified the overall balance of the area. The presentation of this plan discouraged English Partnerships and the local authority from proceeding further.

After this interruption, the process seems to be starting again at the time of writing. All parties are interested in promoting the development of this site and making the most of it, with English

Partnerships and the local authority indicating the need for a long-term strategy for the wider area, into which development of this site could fit.

## Conclusions

### Public transport improvements

The Metro line was running through already built-up areas and has proved not to be a trigger for renewal on its own. Research by the University of Newcastle (TRL, 1993) confirms the findings of an earlier study (TRRL, 1985), that there is no evidence the Metro has had a significant effect on patterns of housing development. Similarly, the Metro reinforces retail development rather than leading it. This public transport connection is seen by developers and employers as a bonus and not as a fundamental criterion for location decisions. Other elements, such as the quality of schools and presence of shops, may be more market-attractive. It is concluded that change is often stimulated by a combination of elements, such as the transport and land use opportunity.

Public transport improvement can be seen as a 'necessary but not sufficient' reason for stimulating interest in the Willington Quay site development opportunity. It would be worth testing elsewhere whether the introduction of a new linear public transport system into a suburban location without good public transport acted as a stronger trigger for housing redevelopment at higher densities.

### Site development opportunities

A second conclusion concerns the need to look outside the site and consider a wider area both in analytical and strategic terms. Limiting the focus to the site makes the change unrealistic in practical terms and would not allow the renewal of a fragmented area. This case also shows that in a complex development situation – with a contaminated brownfield site – there is also a need to promote a partnership approach with other local and national agencies.

Third, this suburban area presents a subtle mixture of local conditions in a substantially stable situation in terms of market potential and infrastructure. Communities are well established in the area but individual families move easily within it. By doing this, they determine micro-processes of decline or regeneration, in an area where housing stock quality and value are often close to the margin.

### Community engagement

Another important aspect refers to the social fabric. This implies that relatively fine grain change is likely to be the type of change which is most likely to occur and succeed. Change should be carefully injected into the urban system and monitored. It is important to use a more patient and incremental approach to suburban renewal. Where an area is in decline, the aim should be to seek action which increases confidence in existing householders as well as investors. Public sector pump priming can seek to change the long-term economic, social and environmental 'trajectory' of the area.

In practical terms, to maximise the opportunities created by development on redundant land, there is a need for four elements:

- a comprehensive analysis of the functional character of this area to determine problems and potentials

- a broad vision for change in the whole area based on local aspirations

- a development framework or brief for the specific site and surrounding areas to integrate the two preceding elements into a realistic partnership-based strategy for change

- a creative approach to individual development opportunities, linked to an ongoing process of effective community support.

**Figure 9.2** Howdon Lane site (reproduced with permission from North Tyneside Council)

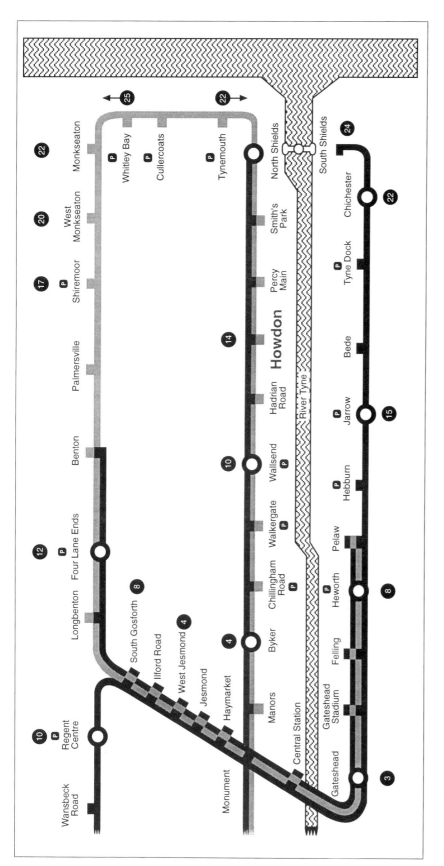

**Figure 9.3 The Tyneside Metro Network (reproduced with permission from Nexus)**

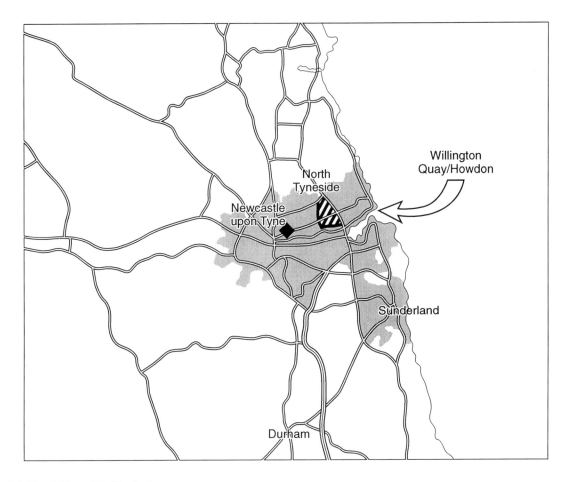

**Figure 9.4 North Tyneside Study Area**

# 10 Community visioning: the Birmingham experience

## Introduction

Constructive community participation has been highlighted as a significant feature of successful regeneration strategies (e.g. Joseph Rowntree Foundation's Action on Estates Programme 1992–95). However, examples of active involvement in the drawing up of a strategy – or vision – for an area are more limited in the context of the more economically robust suburb.

Birmingham City Council is currently pursuing a strategy of local involvement/local action (LILA) to promote local democracy across all wards. This strategy is the result of a long-standing interest in devolution and promotion of participation, and also of the lessons drawn from two pilot devolution projects in the inner city suburb of Aston and the outer suburb of West Northfield. Here we will focus on the latter, exploring the impact of this devolution strategy in terms of promoting local participation and regeneration of the suburbs.

## The pressure for change

West Northfield is the part of the Northfield constituency located in the south-west corner of Birmingham (see Fig. 10.2). It covers partially or entirely four wards amounting to a population of less than 50,000, mainly white (95 per cent compared to 79 per cent city-wide). The other economic and social indicators – from the 1991 Census – are close to the Birmingham average. However, there are significant pockets of deprivation mainly corresponding to a few public housing estates. The distress of these areas is high by Birmingham and national standards. For example, the Leyhill estate is subject to a 40 per cent residents' turnover and one of its schools to more than 60 per cent pupils' turnover.

The area is predominantly residential. Housing was in 1991 equally divided at around 47 per cent between owner-occupied and rented from the local authority. Private and public are sometimes clustered separately (such as respectively in Hanging Lane and Egghill) but in other areas are mixed (Rednall Triangle). Large public housing estates in the Bromsgrove area, formerly outside the boundary of Birmingham City Council, are now included in the city administration. Other housing types are predominantly 1930s–50s terraced or semi-detached. There is a problem of maintenance of some of this ageing housing stock, which cannot always be met by private owners. In some neighbourhoods there is also a question of adapting the houses to growing numbers of elderly or single-parents.

Employment is concentrated in the Rover plant at Longbridge and a few other major firms such as Kalamazoo. The main shopping area is in Northfield Centre along the A38. The centre has thrived in recent years ranking fifth in Birmingham, but is now beginning to suffer, mainly because of traffic congestion. Public transport is a problem in the area, especially in peripheral estates, which are very poorly served.

Several factors have contributed to the changes taking place in this part of Birmingham. The closure of the Rubery/Hollymoor hospital provided a development site of a significant size and an opportunity for the Council to assess local development needs. Ideas for a devolution project were developing in the Council at around the same time. The intention of the Council was to test on the ground devolution ideas which had been circulating for some time. A second implicit aim was to start to look at the regeneration of areas beyond the inner city, which had already been the subject of much attention. West Northfield was selected for the pilot devolution project in 1993. The strategy has now been incorporated in the town-wide LILA.

Local government change requires interconnected elements, ranging from political mechanisms, to management, finance and participation (Sullivan, 1997). The Council identified three principal instruments to take forward the pilot devolution project:

- area sub-committees with members from the Council and local representatives to oversee the activities

- secondment to the project of senior Council officers

- financial mechanisms to promote local involvement.

## Managing change

The area in itself is economically and socially stable, though affected by external or local economic cycles. Change is likely to occur as a result of major re-development on the Rubery/Hollymoor hospital site, which has the potential capacity for between 600 and 700 units of housing.

Together with the devolution component, the Council has concentrated its effort in devising a general regeneration strategy for the area and various initiatives on individual housing estates. The West Northfield Area Regeneration Initiative (WNARI) has been in existence since 1993. Priorities were defined in terms of employment creation on industrial and commercial sites, improvement of public transport provision and local training opportunities. A major consultation exercise undertaken to prepare the strategy, has identified the following key issues:

- taking advantage of the opportunities offered by the new development in the Rubery/Hollymoor hospital site

- more community facilities, especially for young people

- more local open space and improvement of existing spaces

- traffic calming measures

- improvement of safety and security in the area.

Individual regeneration initiatives have focused on the local authority's estates such as Egghill and Shenley Fields. The problems of the first one were identified by an estate profile and a 'planning for real' exercise in 1994. Following these, a development brief, for a site made available by the demolition of the remaining maisonettes, has been prepared in consultation with the relevant agencies. It has been low priority to promote similar improvement strategies, which could be based on local repair teams and advice, for the private housing estates.

In terms of regeneration, the evaluation of the pilot project (Sullivan, 1997) has highlighted that, as a result, greater attention has been paid to the relationship between mainstream service delivery and national regeneration projects. Doubtless, the area focus promoted by the devolution approach helps to concentrate on local solutions. However, because of the complexity of the process, decentralisation of service delivery has proved difficult. Both SRB bids presented in 1995/96 and 1996/97 were unsuccessful.

As seen above, one important component of the strategy has been the promotion of local involvement and participation. The main instrument has been the creation of the *Community Grant* scheme in 1993. This scheme allocated £300,000 to the whole West Northfield area in the first year and now £50,000 per ward. Voluntary and community groups can bid for this fund, one outcome of which is the development of a community and training centre at Rubery. Final decisions on allocations are taken by the representatives of the community and ratified by the area sub-committee which includes Council members. An evaluation of the programme in 1995 by the Institute of Local Government Studies (INLOGOV) (Sullivan, 1997) at the University of Birmingham found that it has been successful in the continuance of many groups, the establishment of new ones and fostering communication between them, both in the public and private housing areas.

The response to the Council efforts in promoting participation in private as well as in public housing areas has been positive. Over time, local community organisations have increased from 48 to 172. Local groups have successfully campaigned and obtained a health centre, the realisation of the community centre, and have raised childcare and transport questions. Another

important achievement relates to the improvement of the communication between the various locally-based or problem-based groups, made possible at some common event such as a community conference and the consultation process linked to the Area Regeneration Initiative. The opportunity to compare agendas allows a clearer perception of shared problems, trade-offs between various issues and positive sum game solutions. This has led to a more positive response to opportunities by local groups in the private housing areas.

Local involvement, level of commitment and participation techniques have varied significantly between neighbourhoods. Table 3 shows how three

**Table 3  Community involvement experiences in Northfield**

| Area | Key characteristics | Community involvement |
| --- | --- | --- |
| Egghill/ Raven Hayes | Public housing estate<br>At the edge of the Birmingham administrative area<br>Predominantly poorly maintained, semi-detached concrete properties<br>Low popularity and some vacancies | *Planning for real*<br>The area has been involved in a 'planning for real' exercise, which has identified problems and possible solutions. In particular the exercise has looked at the renewal of the housing stock and environment, and the opportunities offered by the development of the adjacent ex-hospital site. Some clearance measures are likely to be taken. |
| Rednall Triangle | Located between the A38, the ex-hospital site and the Rover plant<br>Predominantly well maintained and attractive private sector housing<br>Active community groups<br>Stable employment historically linked to Rover<br>An elderly population<br>Some renovation of the housing stock has been undertaken by Bellway, showing that there is a demand for refurbished properties | *Residents' forum*<br>Participation and local involvement has always been high. The area has a very active residents' forum which has fought and obtained a new health centre just north of the area, and has been active in influencing provision of facilities at the ex-hospital site. |
| Hanging Lane | Predominantly private sector housing<br>Located between a golf course and A38<br>Close to the shops of Northfield Centre<br>Suffers from rat-running problems<br>Some housing maintenance problems | *Community organisations*<br>There are a number of community organisations but also a lack of public buildings and meeting places. The local residents have reacted strongly to the traffic congestion and rat-running problems. |

**Figure 10.1 Suburban community planning in action**

areas have reacted differently in terms of participation practice and regeneration strategies.

The evaluation conducted by INLOGOV (Sullivan, 1997) identified some problems of coherence in the implementation of the devolution strategy. Such a strategy requires a considerable degree of political continuity and consensus at the Council level, a constant budget to resource residents' involvement, and a commitment between different service providers within and outside the Council. In addition, the shortage of focal points/catalysts (physical development opportunities, services' re-organisation, transport strategies) on which to concentrate the energy raised by the participation process may frustrate or prevent more far-reaching locally-supported initiatives. The success at West Northfield has been partly because of the focus of re-development at the ex-hospital site, with groups able to influence the range of facilities provided.

## Conclusions

### Community involvement

The two pilot devolution projects have opened the way to the town-wide LILA strategy. Devolution could be a key element in promoting long-term suburban renewal, but it is too early to evaluate the impact.

Participation is essential for the reinforcement of community identity and the shared perception of problems, and identification of relevant solutions. Birmingham City Council has not missed the opportunity to make this an important element of its devolution strategy. It is a pioneering example of local government change applied to suburbs as well as to the inner city. The process which has been initiated is very labour and commitment intensive, and can be incremental and fruitful only in the long term. In addition, transforming local service delivery – which has determined the success of many regeneration programmes – has proved to be controversial. This raises the question of the political nature of such a process.

There is a specific suburban dimension to participation experiments. Suburban problems such as lack of facilities, community centres and focal points, mix of tenure, decaying housing stock, shortage of non-residential uses and poor accessibility, require tailor-made solutions. The shortage of meeting points brings practical problems as does the high degree of human resources required for community support. But, most important, the more dispersed nature of the community and the structural weakness of local organisations mean that public participation is mainly driven by defensive reactions to changes that are perceived as threats, rather than by pro-active initiatives.

## Channelling energies

In the case of stagnant or declining suburbs, consideration should be given to ways to channel the energies raised by participation into positive physical opportunities or management decisions. These opportunities, such as the review of the transport strategy for the area, or the creation of housing repair schemes, will have to be promoted by the Council, local politicians, or more established local groups, businesses and voluntary organisations. At West Northfield the focus of a major re-development opportunity was of considerable importance in involving local people in the renewal of suburban areas.

## Involving the business community

In the West Northfield initiative there was a notable lack of involvement of business groups. Together with participation there is an opportunity to promote a private/public partnership approach in the suburbs, similar to the inner cities. There are relatively few businesses in the suburbs, but the Council has had a great deal of interest from Rover, the largest employer in the area, and from the developers of the Rubery/Hollymoor site. Rover has, for example, recently become involved in childcare provision for the community. Both Parties have been partners in bids put forward to secure financial support from European sources. However, increased involvement and commitment from smaller local businesses and voluntary business organisations would be beneficial to the process, as strong partnership arrangements around regeneration strategies can assist growth and add value, sustainability and ownership to a specific suburb.

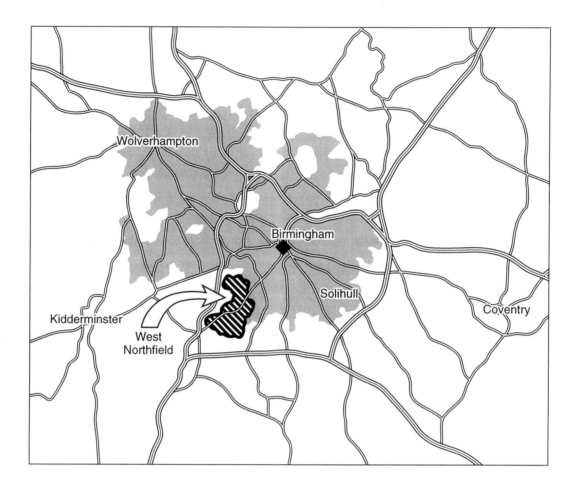

**Figure 10.2  West Northfield Study Area**

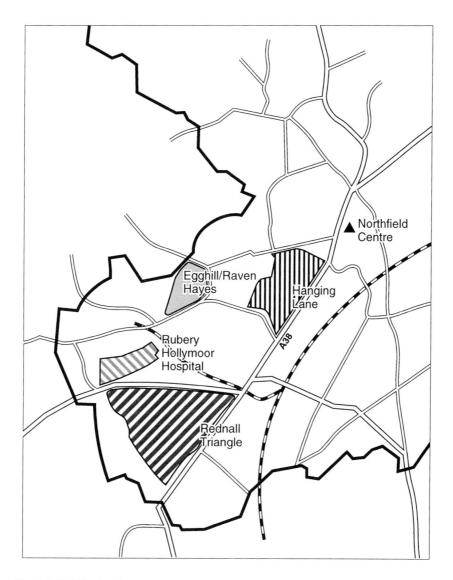

Figure 10.3  West Northfield, Birmingham

# 11 Conclusions

## A neglected field

Our literature review has confirmed that suburbs, as defined in this study, represent a relatively neglected dimension of the urban picture in the UK. A certain amount of theoretical analysis has taken place, and large public sector housing estates have been the subject of considerable attention. The latter have been well documented, especially through the extensive research programmes supported by the Joseph Rowntree Foundation (Action on Estates Programme, 1992–95 and Area Regeneration, 1997 onwards). But, of analysis of changes, threats and opportunities for the suburbs as a whole, there has been very little.

In one sense this is not surprising. The pressing problems of central and inner areas, the immediacy of development decisions and pressures on the urban fringe have naturally commanded priority for most urban local authorities. Faced with these problems it has been reasonable to view existing suburbs as a haven of relative stability and order. It is already clear from our research that many parts of the suburbs do exhibit these and other positive characteristics. In the words of several of those we interviewed, 'they are not a problem'.

In another sense, however, the lack of analysis is disturbing. Suburbs on almost any definition, and certainly on the basis of those definitions we have set out in this research, constitute a major part of our urban fabric, defined both in terms of population accommodation and the scale of land occupied. If we are to make progress with the delivery of an 'Urban Renaissance', as espoused by the Government, then the scope for the suburbs to play a more positive and sustainable role within city regions simply cannot be overlooked.

It is also evident from our studies that the term 'suburb' encompasses a wide range of places and circumstances. Whilst many, indeed the majority of suburbs, may for political and physical reasons offer little scope for change, this still leaves a substantial element where potential probably does exist but remains largely unexplored.

Our interviewees have confirmed the first impression of common problems in suburbia, such as the decay of the housing stock, local centres and facilities, and the shortage of housing and social variety. However, in this analysis, we have gone beyond a generic concept of 'suburbia' and identified six types of suburb. Suburbs have their own history, character and potential. It is around their nature that policies, plans and any interventions should be built. For example, so-called public transport suburbs – which developed around major infrastructural networks – offer an opportunity for improving economic and social sustainability by attracting investment and a mix of functions and residents at public transport nodes. Their level of accessibility is an advantage which should be exploited in imaginative ways. On the other hand, some car suburbs offer potential for improving the environmental and design quality but would require strong intervention to become more sustainable in terms of transport and energy consumption.

Our analysis suggests that specific problems and needs, and consequent physical opportunities for change, probably occur to some degree in many suburbs. Taken together, and over a reasonable period of time, they could constitute a significant challenge and development opportunity. Because, however, they are not often concentrated into a large-scale physical and social 'problem', with the exception of the municipal housing estates, there is a danger that their collective scale and potential contribution will continue to be unappreciated.

## A timely study

There was an almost universal welcome from those we interviewed for our studies. Local authorities were generally aware of problems in some of their suburban areas and wanted to see them set in a wider context. Other players agreed issues needed more attention at the national as well as local level, although they held varying views about both suburban potential and appropriate responses. Time and again we were told that this was a timely study of a neglected dimension.

This timeliness has certainly been increased by the pattern of public debate and political events since we first conceived the project. It has been further reinforced during the period of the study itself. The fierce national debate about housing numbers and their location, resulting in the current 'Urban Renaissance Policy', the evolution of a new 'National Sustainable Development Strategy', the transport debate relating to the 'Transport White Paper' with its call for a gradual change in lifestyles and associated transport patterns, all recognised that the contribution of the suburbs to the 'holistic' and 'integrated' solutions now advocated must be further explored.

But there are other less obvious political dimensions that are equally relevant. The drive for renewed and revitalised local democracy, social inclusion and a sense of community, for example – as reflected in the recent local government White Paper *In Touch with the People* (DETR, 1998a) – is especially relevant to the suburbs.

## Realistic perspectives

It was evident in our discussions that a move towards greater sustainability in the suburbs, accompanied by a degree of renewal and re-development, would imply, to many people, wholesale change and major physical restructuring. Such a large-scale change, certainly in the short term, would be impractical in political and economic terms. The physical scope in many cases is limited, fragmented ownership makes for difficulties, and the political will is not evident locally or nationally. It is unrealistic to think that the suburbs will provide a quick and easy answer to our housing and sustainability problems. They could, however, make a significant contribution to meeting housing need, gradually and over time, if

a package of fine grain interventions were put in place, to trigger change. We return to this point later.

A further key message of the research is that many suburbs are likely to justify attention primarily because of their own problems and needs, rather than simply being considered as contributors to housing or other strategic requirements. Problems of ailing local centres, community facilities, poor choice of transport and in particular local housing needs will often be of genuine concern to local people and their politicians. They provide a basis, therefore, for engagement and for a process of community planning. As confidence develops over a reasonable period of time and some successes occur, scope for other projects – for example, additional housing renewal, selective re-development and some new mixes of uses – should grow.

To simply 'impose' housing development quotas on a suburb, without engaging with its local community and its problems, is, however, likely simply to create a resistance and increase the weariness and hostility with which some suburban communities already tend to react to proposals for change and development. It is also important not to confuse self-sufficiency for suburbs with sustainability, when considering topics like local employment. Suburbs such as Redbridge in London are part of a much larger employment market. But they can nevertheless become more sustainable in other ways.

Finally, our analysis of foreign experiences has helped us to understand how it is possible to improve suburban areas in sustainability terms. The American, Canadian and Australian cases of re-development and suburb-wide planning have now helped to transform many shapeless and decaying suburbs. The US experience in particular has promoted a more pro-active and 'visionary' approach to suburban policy, involving local communities. From practice in Continental Europe it is possible to learn how to introduce a greater mix of uses and environmental sustainability, especially in terms of transport, and how to make suburbs integrated with the rest of the urban structure. However, these experiences cannot simply be transferred to the UK context. There is a need to consider how some elements of these strategies can be adapted to local UK situations. The following sections therefore present our responses to this question, grouped under four headings:

- positive planning

- scope for action

- urban management and community involvement

- further studies.

## Positive planning

A combination of broad analysis/strategy and locally tailored, fine grain interventions was not generally evident in the case studies. Although there was, in all case studies, a reasonable level of awareness and concern, collective corporate responses were not particularly evident and a shortage of political interest was apparent.

The exception was the Birmingham Northhills area, where the establishment of a clear community focus, driven by politicians and accompanied by a desire for strong corporate co-ordination, offers the potential for effective neighbourhood planning and a more creative approach. Hopefully the new initiatives in North Bristol will follow a similar path. The case in North Tyneside shows the importance of positive planning in terms of the emerging need of a comprehensive analysis of the area to determine problems and potentials. A purely site-specific focus taking advantage of land availability and good transport connections has proved difficult to implement. A comprehensive analysis would allow preparation of a development

framework for the wider area and the promotion of an effective partnership approach.

The Redbridge experience in London highlights that a strategic vision of the future of issues such as retailing in suburban areas is now needed. This case demonstrates the difficulty of maintaining or promoting more mixed uses and self-contained communities in metropolitan areas, where the high level of accessibility and movement has enabled segregation of uses rather than integration, especially in the suburbs. Positive planning in Redbridge requires a comprehensive strategy, covering land use, public and private transport, parking, re-development and infill.

Recent planning experiences in Portland, Vancouver and Seattle have shown how a pro-active role from the local authority and all sectors of the community in devising a strategy for suburban areas can be successful in renewing the suburbs, reflecting sustainability criteria. The ingredients of these strategies involve: a strong local economic and community dimension, wide public and private involvement, promotion of innovative public transport, and selective small-scale re-development. More important, the definition and combination of these ingredients has shaped community plans and vision documents, which provide a framework for intervention and collective expectations.

The ingredients for suburban strategies and plans should vary case by case. As a general framework, the complete 'shopping list' would include:

- **increase of mix of uses**

- **re-design of suburban centres**

- **re-development of brownfield sites or urban voids**

- **selective densification of housing**

- **sustainable transport (especially buses, cycle and pedestrian networks)**

- **regional planning (connecting the suburb to a polycentric urban system)**

- **participation and community involvement**

- **improved urban design guidance**

- **environmental and green space improvements**

- **housing maintenance improvements, and mix of tenure and types**

- **more efficient and accessible facilities and public services.**

It is clear that the suburbs are vital components of the urban mix in economic, social, political and environmental terms. They are dynamic and changing. If that change is to be encouraged and managed in directions which reflect local and national policy, it will require a local authority and its partners to create an enabling strategic framework, rather than reacting in a passive way.

The promotion of a more positive approach to suburban renewal can be addressed via the development planning system. In general, the formal Development Plans that were examined took a rather passive view of the suburbs, given modest encouragement to issues such as house conversion or some changes of use of district centres, but saying little about other opportunities. The majority of the development control policies are couched in negative terms. The authorities recognise the need to review and update their plans, but the process has proved very slow in the past and needs to be accelerated. Policies for a particular suburb should also be set in a district, and increasingly regional, context.

In establishing a more positive planning framework, more attention needs to be given to sustainability criteria, making use of the analysis that is set out in the first part of this study (particularly Chapter 4). The criteria are not immutable laws, but they are a useful guide and

they need to be more consciously woven into future decisions.

Bournemouth provides an interesting example of an authority which has had to deal with strong housing market pressures for suburban development for some time, and has responded with a suite of policies in its Local Plan. Some, though not all, are of a positive stance and a considerable scale of re-development and intensification has occurred.

Other agencies need to be drawn more actively into the processes by local authorities. The health authorities, transport operators and utility companies can all make decisions about provision which can crucially affect the quality of life and sustainability considerations in suburbs. Yet our limited analysis suggests their decisions are at best poorly integrated and are made with scant regard to wider sustainability issues. Relocation of a health centre to a suburban centre or promoting mixed use schemes on redundant utility sites could have a powerful impact. Where they exist in suburbs the local business communities also need to be drawn into the process, something which did not occur much in Northfield. Programmes like the 'New Deal Programme' and the LGA's 'New Commitment Initiative' should help but these processes are currently to be focused on only a relatively few 'core' regeneration areas and will need to be applied more widely in the suburbs.

Good design guidance can also help to identify opportunities, provide reassurance and demonstrate a commitment to quality. Good design guidance and support is however of little use in isolation. The political and community context has to be developed in parallel or, better, in advance. But design guidance can help identify opportunities, provide reassurance and demonstrate a commitment to quality which can assist the process of change and improve the outcomes. Bodies such as the recently formed Urban Design Alliance (UDAL) might, therefore, be encouraged to work with appropriate local authorities at the LGA to produce appropriate design guidance focused particularly on suburbs.

Environment and ecology in the suburbs are not commonly seen as being deficient. However, there is also an opportunity to improve the level of environmental sustainability in much of the urban areas by well-focused policies. The thinking now devised for eco-villages, energy conservation in buildings, waste and water consumption minimisation, green corridors and so on can be widely applied to the suburbs. The recent experience in Leicester on energy efficiency shows what is possible.

Finally, professions involved in the built environment, the urban and housing realm – ranging from planners, architects, environmentalists, social and economic experts – should be challenged to re-think the suburb. Urban models and policies are usually devised for new developments or inner cities. The suburb should become more central to this thinking. There is for these professions scope to propose imaginative community renewal strategies for the UK suburbs.

## Scope for action

To illustrate the scope we believe exists we have set out below four examples of suburban issues which can bring together both local concerns and the application of sustainability principles, and make a contribution to wider needs.

### Transport integration

In all the study areas a relatively good public transport network exists, focused primarily on radial routes. It is, however, in large part a 'historic' network that has adapted surprisingly little to changing circumstances. This lack of change and impact has clearly contributed to marked increases in car usage found in all the study areas. Whilst investment in fixed track, high-capacity linear

systems such as the Tyneside Metro and the proposed Bristol LRT are useful, the prime challenge relates to re-shaping the bus network and creating safe cycle and pedestrian facilities. This requires relatively modest levels of investment, but could help suburbs restore the more balanced choice of transport that has actually been lost in many areas over the last 30 years. As highlighted by this research, in this field there is much to learn from 'transit-oriented development' and 'pedestrian pockets' experiences in the United States and transport policies in Continental Europe.

### Local centres

Although we were aware of the problem of decline in smaller suburban shopping centres and parades prior to the study, we were nevertheless struck by both the recurrence in that problem, and the extent to which such centres were seen by local people as very important focal points of community activity and identity. This was further reinforced during the course of the study by a local community group from *Oxford* who contacted the Civic Trust to help arrest the decline of their local centre, which they saw as the key to the community's future. It is, however, evident that the economic forces creating the decline of some, although by no means all, suburban centres are powerful and in some cases probably irreversible. Nevertheless, the local authority response is often piecemeal and unconvincing. The Civic Trust's wider 'Centre Vision' programme (report to be published early 1999) makes the case for a more positive and co-ordinated local authority intervention, working with local people. We have included in the Appendices, therefore, an illustration of how such an approach might take place in respect of the *Gants Hill* area in the London Borough of Redbridge (Figure 8.8). This is of course only an initial study and only one example of the potential we believe exists.

## Community facilities

The need for better community facilities and support in parts of the suburbs was also a recurring theme. Older or ageing community facilities, often transformed from another use, can be costly to run and make poor use of available sites. Some existing public leisure facilities in suburbs are run down or simply not available. PPP or PFI finance may be available for re-developing these sites for housing and/or community and leisure facilities such as indoor tennis and bowls courts. These issues have been partly addressed in recent publications by LPAC and other studies.

## Housing renewal and adaptation

In the case studies, substantial brownfield sites, ripe for development, were the exception rather than the rule, and we believe this will be reflected more widely. We have already also mentioned the impracticality of re-developing substantial elements of existing suburban housing. In addition, some parts of the suburban housing stock that we examined are visibly ageing and selective replacement may well need to be contemplated in the fairly near future, together with encouragement to private owners to maintain property in good repair. Consideration should be given to the re-introduction of 'Housing Improvement Grants'. In the meantime, we believe that local authorities could stimulate appropriate property conversions, including the provision of more accommodation for the elderly, new 'LOTS' initiatives, housing repair advice and selective re-development of sites in or close to declining local centres and greenspaces, that could be served by public transport. Such schemes, focused on design principles advanced by the Urban Design Alliance and recent studies by Llewelyn-Davies (1998) and others, would need to be essentially privately funded, but the authorities would need to consider using their power to assist land assembly in some circumstances. The Government's current review of these land assembly and purchase powers may assist. Car

parking standards and other access considerations will also need to be reviewed as proposed in the recent suite of studies for LPAC referred to earlier.

Many interviewees have indicated that there is a mismatch between types of housing available in the suburbs and demand. This mismatch is a result of the changing structure of the population, with more elderly, single people and small families compared to the time when suburbs where built. However, many suburbanites are very attached to their neighbourhood and would not like to move far from it. The challenge is to encourage and support *a fine grain* type of intervention. Housing variety should be created within the existing suburban fabric by careful small-scale change; a process of re-stitching. In the short term, the amount of new housing created by these changes would be relatively modest, but the collective contribution of suburbs as a whole, taken nationally, could nevertheless be significant. Furthermore, if such projects are successful, they could provide a platform for other rather more substantial forms of housing re-development at a later date, when suburban ageing has reached a new pitch.

## Urban management and community involvement

The studies demonstrate a need for some suburbs to adapt better to meet perceived local needs and pressures, and there is useful scope for them to do so in a manner which allows some physical adaptation, reverses current trends towards suburban insustainability, and provides a positive response to wider housing and 'Urban Renaissance' needs. Little of this will happen, however, without effective community engagement and involvement. Yet it was repeatedly emphasised to us that such activities are resource hungry, and that local authorities are under severe pressure and face greater social priorities elsewhere within their area. Most of the suburbs we are considering do not qualify for special grants or assistance. How is this conundrum to be addressed?

The starting point is to recognise that community engagement is a long-term process and a gradual one. JRF's research programmes have repeatedly demonstrated this lesson, but the case studies show it will also apply to predominantly owner-occupied suburbs as well. This does not, therefore, require a sudden flood of community development resources, but rather a steady trickle of such investments, building up capacity and confidence over time. The second point is to recognise that much of that investment will need to come from outside the local authorities, from the voluntary and business sectors and the local community itself. (We do, however, later suggest a way in which those resources could be augmented at the local level.) A third factor is the need for the authority to see the issue as a corporate matter, part of moves towards new devolved forms of urban management, yet also linked clearly to its strategic role and strategic needs. Collectively the authorities' available resources can be greater than is often assumed. The authority needs to see it also as a part of its response to the Government's requirement to revitalise local democracy and create a new sense of active citizenship and civic pride. Encouragingly, both Birmingham and Bristol have already embarked on this difficult journey.

Given the importance of this bundle of issues the relative scale of resources required should not be insuperable. The Government should now consider ways of encouraging such a process, especially as it is one they clearly regard in the round as critical. A number of suggestions are made in the recommendations.

The outcome of such a strengthened process would be a better community understanding of the processes of physical and other change affecting suburbs, and we believe the confidence to develop a more creative response. Simple, clear, focused Community Action Plans and programmes would result, and would foster a process of gradual

adaptation and change, a *'re-stitching and re-tailoring of the urban fabric'* – a process of positive management rather than benign neglect.

To assist the process it would be appropriate to consider importing into the suburb two elements drawn from rural experience. One is the notion of 'urban parishing', allowing a given suburb powers to raise a modest rate which will be ring-fenced for community development programmes and purposes. As Government has recently agreed that there will be BIDS (business improvements districts) with modest money-raising powers, why not a community equivalent in the suburbs – CIDS (community improvement districts)! Rural areas already enjoy these powers. The second is the use of 'community appraisals', currently being promoted by the Housing Corporation in relation to affordable housing in rural communities.

Further scope may also be created by the use of funds from the Lottery 'New Opportunities Fund' for community purposes.

## Further studies

The suburbs that we studied, and some of our other research, suggested that a basic framework of community activity and consciousness often exists. In some suburbs, or parts of suburbs (and not only in the more prosperous areas), it has already reached a high level, and a response to the new challenge should be relatively easy. We see this sense of community as a vital resource, a form of capital, *'social capital'* quite as valuable as *'environmental capital'* or traditional forms of capital investment. There is certainly now a need to understand better this concept of *social capital*, what makes it form, what sustains it and what are the critical levels for a healthy community. We can then perhaps use it as a 'litmus' of community health. Then, when *social capital* is seen to be low or declining, preventative action could be taken before matters become critical. We see this concept, which itself needs further study, as especially relevant to suburbs, where at present a gradual deterioration in social capital may not be recognised until decay is well advanced.

Although the sample of case studies has proved useful, we have been conscious that it represents a relatively small test of the suburban dimension in a national context. We were also unable to pursue solutions to issues identified in sufficient depth to produce fully worked up proposals. We believe there is, therefore, now a need to extend the research, both through an enlarged sample of suburbs, especially in middle-sized towns, and, second, to pursue a small number of pilot projects which would allow specific proposals to be pursued in depth and hopefully implemented. There is in particular a clear need to review the conditions and quality of the ageing housing and infrastructure in older suburbs, in order to assess future need for renewal. This view has been reinforced by two unsolicited appeals made to the Civic Trust during the course of the study. One already mentioned was from a voluntary group in *Oxford* concerned about the declining facilities and future of their suburb and its sense of community. The other was an approach by *Reading Borough Council* which has already identified the need to undertake more investigations into the potential for gradual renewal of some of its suburbs, both in an 'Urban Renaissance' context, and in order to improve facilities for local residents. We believe that these two contacts represent the tip of a considerable iceberg of potential interest and demand.

# 12 Recommendations

That *Government* recognises the importance of the potential suburban contribution to *its urban renaissance, sustainability, social cohesion and democracy policies* and accordingly:

- encourages local authorities to develop positive, community-based programmes for their suburban areas

- requires local authorities to incorporate appropriate positive policies in their development plans

- supports the development of a pilot initiatives programme

- introduces 'urban parishing' linked to appropriate powers to raise a modest 'parish' rate for community development purposes

- considers the introduction of a national 'community chest' to supplement local funds for community development

- supports the introduction of 'community appraisals', mirroring their successful application in rural areas.

That the *Local Government Association* encourages greater awareness of the suburban dimension and the spread of good practice in responding to community needs and unlocking potential.

That *local authorities* with significant suburban areas:

- adopt pro-active community-based plans and programmes for those areas, rooted in community needs and sustainable development principles

- that service co-ordination is improved to facilitate this process, drawing in other agencies

- that development plans reflect a more positive and creative approach to selective suburban renewal and redevelopment.

That the *voluntary sector* be helped to assist the community process in suburbs at the local level, and to increase awareness at a national level.

That the *Urban Design Alliance* be encouraged to produce guidance specifically targeted on design and development opportunities in suburban areas.

That *other agencies*, such as transport operators, health authorities and public utilities, be encouraged to play a more positive part in suburban evolution.

That the *Joseph Rowntree Foundation* considers supporting a wider range of case studies of suburbs, especially in medium-sized towns, together with the further development of appropriate criteria for assessing suburban sustainability.

That a limited number of pilot initiatives in suburban areas be tested and developed, in order to demonstrate the scope for incremental renewal – the pilots to focus particularly on restructuring district and community centres, and the scope for associated transport improvements and housing provision for smaller households.

# Appendix 3: Semi-structured interview format and interviewees

## Semi-structured interviews

1.  What do you understand by the term 'suburban'?

    Does this have a particular meaning in the UK context as opposed to abroad?

    What are the main differences between the UK model and elsewhere?

2.  Do you think that 'suburbia', as we knew/know it, is being re-defined?

    If yes, then how – what are the main trends?

3.  What are the main pressures for change? Distinguish between exogenous and indigenous catalysts.

    What are the constraints?

4.  How significant do you think the issue of 'sustainable development' is in the re-interpretation of suburbs?

    What kind of responses/case studies do you know of where the drive for 'sustainable renewal' of a suburban area has led to direct intervention of some kind.

5.  Are there key lessons which can be learnt from UK and/or international experience which can be adapted/imported to a number of locations?

6.  Are you aware of any specific measures (particularly policy-related measures) which have facilitated renewal in suburban areas?

7.  Which types of suburban area do you think exhibit most potential for renewal and why? Over what timescale?

## Semi-structured interviews were conducted with

Professor Allan Cochrane
Faculty of Social Science
Open University

Professor Michael Breheny
Department of Geography
University of Reading

Christine Lambert
Faculty of the Built Environment
University of the West of England

Professor Duncan Maclennan
Department of Urban Studies
University of Glasgow

David Bannister
Department of Planning
The Bartlett School, University College London

John Montgomery
Director
Urban Cultures Ltd

Robert Vaughan
Group Property
NatWest Group

Bill Stevenson
Director
Bellway plc

David Coates
Planning and Technical Director
House Builders Federation

David Lunts
Chief Executive
Urban Villages Forum

# Appendix 4: Advisory Panel members

Greg Clark, Head of Economic Development, Greater London Enterprise

Dr Peter Newman, School of the Built Environment, University of Westminster

Martin Pope, Head of Town Planning, Boots The Chemists

John Montgomery, Director, Urban Cultures

Les Sparks, Head of Planning, Birmingham City Council

Ian Womack, Property Director, Norwich Union

Alf Strange, Director, Land Securities Properties

# Appendix 5: Case study forum format

**Case study: format for focus group meetings**

Introduction from the research team.

**Context**

- Origin of suburban area under study.

- Recent history and identification of main 'driver(s)' for change.

- Reasons for this 'change'.

- Differing levels of involvement from officers/members present at focus group.

**Evidence of impact on surrounding area in terms of**

- Economic mix, e.g. development of new foci of employment.

- Environmental quality, e.g. associated with change car dependency/public transport.

- Social cohesion, security and safety.

- Housing – tenure, quality, mix, condition, etc.

**Managing the change**

- Extent to which pressure for change has been integrated into plans for a different settlement pattern, e.g. has it been associated with a specific development brief or master plan for the area, did this happen pre- or post- main change?

- Which departments have been involved in what aspect of re-development/re-appraisal?

- Extent to which the re-interpretation of the study area allows it to respond to principles of sustainable development: economic/environmental/social. Specifically, housing.

- Role of local community (residents/business).

**Constraints and opportunities**

- What constraints have been experienced to date?

- What opportunities are there to further develop the suburban area in question?

- To what extent could these ideas be imported elsewhere?

- How could this be achieved and who should take responsibility?

# Bibliography

## Government guidance

Planning Policy Guidance Note 3 (1992) *Housing*

Planning Policy Guidance Note 13 (1994) *Transport*

Planning Policy Guidance Note 13 (1995) *A Guide to Better Practice*

Planning Policy Guidance Note 6 (1996) *Town Centres and Retail*

Planning Policy Guidance Note 1 (1997) *General Policy and Principles*

## Literature review – sustainable suburbia

Aldous, T. (1992) *Urban Villages*. London: Urban Villages Group

Angotti, T. (1993) *Metropolis 2000: Planning, Poverty and Politics*. London: Routledge

Breheny, M. (ed.) (1992) *Sustainable Development and Urban Form*. London: Pion

Breheny, M. (1993) 'Planning and the sustainable city region', *Town and Country Planning*, Vol. 62, No. 4, pp. 71–4

Brown, M.G. (1995) 'Will Stapleton take off?', *Landscape Architecture*, August

CAG (Consultants Antonia House) (1997) *Sustainable Regeneration Criteria and Barriers*. A Discussion Paper, published. London: CAG Consultants

Calthorpe, P. (1993) *The Next American Metropolis, Ecology Community and the American Dream*. New York: Princeton Architectural Press

Cervero, R. (1986) 'Unlocking suburban gridlock', *Journal of the American Planning Association*, Vol. 52, No. 4, pp. 389–406

Cervero, R. (1995) 'Stockholm's new towns', *Cities*, Vol. 12, No. 6, pp. 41–51

Cheshire, P.C. and Hay, D.G. (1989) *Urban Problems in Western Europe: An Economic Analysis*. London: Unwin Hyman

Chesterton *et al.* (1995) *Dwelling Provision through Planned Regeneration*. Hertfordshire County Council

City of Portland (1993) *Growing Better. A Report to the Planning Commission on Phase I of the Liveable City Project*. Portland: Bureau of Planning

City of Vancouver (1995) *City Plan: Directions for Vancouver*. Vancouver: Planning Department

Civic Trust (1994) *Caring for our Towns and Cities*. Nottingham: Boots the Chemist

Civic Trust (1998) *Dwellings Over and In Shops in London*. London: LAPC

Crockett, D. (1990) 'Suburban redevelopment. An appraisal of recent pressures and policy responses in an outer London borough', *The Planner*, 10 August, pp. 11–14

DETR (Department of the Environment, Transport and the Regions) (1998) *Opportunities for Change: Consultation Paper on a Revised UK Strategy for Sustainable Development*. London: HMSO

DETR (1998a) *Modern Local Government In Touch with the People*. London: HMSO

Downs, A. (1973) *Opening up the Suburbs: An Urban Strategy for America*. New Haven and London: Yale University Press

Duany, A. and Plater-Zyberk, E. (1991) *Town and Town-making Principles*. New York: Rizzoli

Elkin, T., McLaren, D. and Hillman, M. (1991) *Reviving the City: Towards Sustainable Urban Development*. London: Friends of the Earth

Elliot, D. (1996) *The Future of Green Belt and Urban Fringe Issues*. Thesis. London: University of Westminster

European Commission (1990) *Green Paper on the Urban Environment*. Luxembourg: Commission of the European Communities

European Commission (1996) *European Sustainable Cities*. Luxembourg: Office for the Official Publications of the European Community

Foxworthy, R. (1997) *Looking at Neighborhoods – Observations from Successful Neighborhoods in Seattle*. Paper presented at the APA Conference in Contrasts and Transition, San Diego and published on the WWW

Garreau, J. (1991) *Edge City: Life on the New Frontier*. New York: Doubleday

Godwin, C. (1979) *The Oak Park Strategy*. Chicago: University of Chicago Press

Halcrow Fox (February 1998) *Future Sources of Large Scale Housing Land in London*. London: LPAC

Hall, P. (1989) *London 2001*. London: Unwin Hyman

Hall, P. and Hay, D.G. (1980) *Growth Centres in the European Urban System*. London: Heinemann

Haungton, G. and Hunter, C. (1994) *Sustainable Cities*. London: Regional Studies Association

Heidemij (1995) *Urban Environment and Sustainable Development*. Proceedings of the conference 'Towards a new development approach', Brussels, 24–5 November 1994

Hinshaw, M.L. (1989) *Transforming a Suburb*. Proceedings of the Tenth Annual International Pedestrian Conference, Boulder, Colorado, pp. 81–9

Jackson, A.A. (1973) *Semi-detached London. Suburban Development, Life and Transport 1900–39*. Didcot: Wild Swan

Jacobs, J. (1961) *Death and Life of Great American Cities*. Harmondsworth: Penguin

Jacobs, J. (1996) *Edge of Empire, Post Colonialism and the City*. London: Routledge

Katz, P. (1992) *The New Urbanism: Towards an Architecture of Community*. New York: McGraw-Hill

Kelbaugh, D. (ed.) (1989) *The Pedestrian Pocket Book*. New York: Princeton Architectural Press

Knox, P. (1982) *Urban Social Geography*. London: Longman

Leccese, M. (1992) 'Edge city', *Landscape Architecture*, Vol. 82, No. 6, pp. 60–5

Lindgren, H. (1995) 'Bourgeois dystopias', *Landscape Architecture*, August, pp. 51–5

Llewelyn-Davies (1997) *Exploring the Urban Potential for Housing: Manual and Toolkit*. North West Regional Association

Llewelyn-Davies (January 1998) *Sustainable Residential Quality: New Approaches to Urban Living*. London: LPAC

Lock, D. (1994) 'Sustainable patterns of development' *Town and Country Planning*, September, pp. 236–8

London Property Research (October 1996) *Office to other Uses*. London: LPAC

LPAC (London Planning Advisory Committee) (1996) *Supplementary Advice on the Strategic Network and Policy for Town Centres in London*. Committee Report U/8/96. London: LPAC

Montgomery, J. (1998) 'Making a city: urbanity, vitality and urban design', *Journal of Urban Design*, Vol. 3, No. 1, pp. 93–116

Muller, P.O. (1976) *The Outer City*. Resource Paper 22. Washington DC: Association of American Geographers

Mumford, L. (1961) *The City in History*. Harmondsworth: Penguin

Newman, P. and Kenworthy, J. (1989) *Cities and Automobile Dependence*. Aldershot: Gower

Newman, P., Kenworthy, J. and Vintila, P. (1995) 'Can we overcome automobile dependence? Physical planning in an age of urban cynicism', *Cities,* Vol. 12, No. 1, pp. 53–65

Ove Arup and Partners (1998*) Planning for Sustainable Development: Towards Better Practice.* London: HMSO

Palen, J.J. (1995) *The Suburbs.* New York: McGraw Hill

Park, R., Burgess, E. and McKenzie, R. (1925) (eds) *The City.* Chicago: University of Chicago Press

P.S. Martin Hamlin (March 1998) *Housing Requirements of One Person.* London: LPAC

Pucher, J. and Clorer, S. (1992) 'Taming the automobile in Germany', *Transportation Quarterly,* Vol. 46, No. 3, pp. 383–95

Schneider, M. and Fernandez, F. (1989) 'The emerging suburban service economy. Changing patterns of employment', *Urban Affairs Quarterly,* Vol. 24, No. 4, pp. 537–55

Schnore, L.F. (1963) 'The social and economic characteristics of American suburbs', *Sociological Quarterly ,* Vol. 4, pp. 122–34

Southworth, M. and Owens, P.M. (1993) 'The evolving metropolis. Studies of community, neighbourhood and street form at the urban edge', *APA Journal,* Summer, pp. 271–87

Spectorsky, A.C. (1957) *The Exurbanites.* New York: Berkley

Statura, J.M. (1987) 'Suburban socio-economic status change: a comparison of models 1950–1980', *American Sociological Review,* Vol. 52, pp. 268–77

TCPA (1996) *The People: Where Will They Go?* London: TCPA

TCPA (1998) *Urban Housing Capacity: What Can be Done?* London: TCPA

Thorns, D.C. (1972) *Suburbia.* London: McGibbon and Kee

Untermann, R.K. (1984) *Accommodating the Pedestrian. Adapting Towns and Neighborhoods for Walking and Bicycling.* New York: Van Nostrand Reinhold

Van den Berg, L. *et al.* (1982) 'A study of growth and decline', in L. van den Berg *et al.* (eds) *Urban Europe.* Oxford: Pergamon for the European Co-ordination Centre for Research and Documentation in Social Sciences

Van der Ryn, S. and Calthorpe, P. (1986) *Sustainable Communities. A New Design Synthesis for Cities, Suburbs and Towns.* San Francisco: Sierra Club Books

Walker, R. (1981) 'A theory of suburbanization: capitalism and the construction of urban space in the United States', in M. Dear and A.J. Scott (eds*) Urbanization and Urban Planning in Capitalist Society.* London: Methuen

Ward, C. (1989) *Welcome Thinner City: Urban Survival in the 1990s.* London: Bedford Square Press

## Further reading on sustainable suburbia

Baldassare, M. (1986) *Trouble in Paradise: The Suburban Transformation in America.* New York: Columbia University Press

Barnett, J. (1993) 'Sustainable development: how to make it work', *Architectural Record,* Vol. 6, pp. 32–5

Barnett, R. (1978) 'The libertarian suburb', *Landscape,* Vol. 22, No. 3, pp. 44–8

Birrell, R. (1991) 'Infrastructure costs on the urban fringe: Sydney and Melbourne compared' in Economic Planning Advisory Council (ed.) *Background Paper 10.* Canberra: Australian Government Publishing Service

Blowers, A. (ed.) *Planning for a Sustainable Environment.* London: Earthscan

*Built Environment* (1992) Special issue on the compact city, Vol. 18, No. 4

Burns, E.K. (1980) 'The enduring and affluent suburb', *Landscape*, Vol. 24, No. 1, pp. 33–41

Calthorpe, P. and Mack, M. (1989) 'Pedestrian pockets: new strategies for suburban growth' in Kelbaugh, D. (ed.) *The Pedestrian Pocket Book: A New Suburban Design Strategy.* New York: Princeton Architectural Press

Cervero, R. (1989) *America's Suburban Centers: The Land Use Transportation Link.* Boston: Unwin Hyman

Charlesworth, J. and Cochrane, A. (1994) 'Tales of the suburbans: the local politics of growth in the South-East of England', *Urban Studies*, Vol.10, pp. 1723–38

Cholden, H., Hanson, C. and Bohren, R. (1980) 'Suburban status instability' *American Sociological Review*, Vol. 45, pp. 972–83

Council on Environmental Quality (1975) 'The costs of sprawl in the USA', *Ekistics*, Vol. 40, No. 239, pp. 266–72

Council for the Protection of Rural England (CPRE) (1998) *Urban Exodus.* A Report prepared by T. Champion *et al.* for the CPRE. London: CPRE

Dowall, D. (1994) *The Suburban Squeeze: Land Conversion and Regulation in San Francisco Bay Area.* Berkeley: University of California Press

Engwicht, D. (1992) *Towards an Eco-city: Calming the Traffic.* Sydney: Envirobook

Fishman, R. (1987) *Bourgeois Utopias: The Rise and Fall of Suburbia.* New York: Basic Books

Gans, H. (1967) *The Lewittowners: Ways of Life and Politics in a new Suburban Community.* New York: Pantheon Books

Girardet, H. (1992) *Cities: New Directions for Sustainable Urban Living.* London: Gaia Books

Glancey, J. (1994) 'No man's land', *The Independent,* 14 April

Gottmann, J. and Harper, R.A. (1967) *Metropolis on the Move: Geographers Look at Urban Sprawl.* New York: John Wiley

Groth, P. (1988) 'Streetgrids as frameworks for urban variety', *Harvard Architecture Review*, Spring, pp. 68–75

Hall, P. (1992) 'East Thames corridor. The second golden age of the garden suburb', *Urban Design Quarterly*, July

Hooper, A. (1994) 'Land availability and the suburban option', *Town and Country Planning*, Vol. 63, No. 9, pp. 239–42

Hough, M. (1990) *Out of Place. Restoring Identity to the Regional Landscape.* New Haven and London: Yale University Press

Jackson, K.T. (1985) The Suburbanisation of the United States. New York: Oxford University Press

Johnson, J.H. (1974) *Suburban Growth. Geographical Processes at the Edge of the Western City.* London: Wiley & Sons

Langdon, P. (1994) *A Better Place to live: Reshaping the American Suburb.* Amherst: University of Massachusetts Press

Lynch, K. (1960) *The Imaging of the City.* Cambridge, MA: Technology Press and Harvard University Press

Lynch, K. (1976) *Managing the Sense of a Region,* Cambridge, MA: MIT Press

Martin, A.M. and Doak, A.J. (1995) *Consensus Building for Environmental Sustainability: The Case of Lancashire.* Proceedings of the International Sustainable Development Research Conference, Manchester, 27–8 March. Shipley: ERP Environment

Morris, W. and Kaufman, J.A. (1996) *Mixed Used Development – New Designs for New Lifestyles – A Primer for Developers, Planners, Regulators, Builders, Consumers and Small Business People.* Brisbane: Queensland Department of Tourism

Mumsford, L. (1963) *The Highway and the City.* London: Secker and Warburg

Newman, P. and Mouritz, M. (1991) 'Ecologically sustainable urban development and the future of Perth', *Urban Futures*, Vol. 34, No. 2, pp. 13–27

Oliver, P., Davis, I. and Bentley, I. (1981) (eds) *Dunroamin. The Suburban Semi and its Enemies.* London: Pimlico

Orki, C.K. (1985) 'Suburban mobility: the coming transportation crisis?', *Transportation Quarterly*, Vol. 39, No. 2, pp. 283–96

Popenhoe, D. (1977) *The Suburban Environment. Sweden and the United States.* Chicago and London: The University of Chicago Press

RAC/Civic Trust/University of Westminster (1998) *Civilising Cities: the Contribution of Transport and Land use.* London: RAC Motoring Services

Rothblatt, D.N. and Garr, D.J. (1986) *Suburbia: An International Assessment.* New York: St Martin's Press

Rowe, C. (1993) 'USA La periferia come centro urbano' (with English translation), *L'Arca*, December, pp. 4–9

Rowe, P. (1991) *Making a Middle Landscape.* Cambridge, MA: MIT Press

Rowley, A. (1996) *Mixed Used Development: Concept and Realities.* London: RICS

Searle, G. (1991) 'Successes and failures of urban consolidation in Sydney', *Urban Futures*, special issue 1, July, pp. 23–30

Sherlock, H. (1990) *Cities are Good for Us. The Case for High Densities, Friendly Streets, Local Shops and Public Transport.* London: Transport 2000

Southworth, M. and Ben-Joseph, E. (1993) *Regulated Streets: The Evolution of Standards for Suburban Residential Streets.* Working paper. Berkeley: Institute of Urban and Regional Development, University of California

Stilgoe, J.R. (1982) 'Suburbanites forever. The American dream endures', *Landscape Architecture*, May, pp. 89–93

Stilgoe, J.R. (1983) 'Hobgolin in suburbia. Origins of place consciousness', *Landscape Architecture*, November–December, pp. 54–61

Stilgoe, J.R. (1988) *Borderland: Origins of the American Suburb 1820–1939.* New Haven: Yale University Press

Sudjic, D. (1994) 'Nightmare in Acacia Avenue', *The Guardian*, 14 April

Whitehand, J.W.R. (1989) 'Development pressure, development control and suburban townscape change. Case studies in the South East England', *Town Planning Review*, Vol. 60, No. 4, pp. 403–20

Wood, R.C. (1958) *Suburbia. Its People and Their Politics.* Houghton: The Riverside Press Cambridge

**Case study: North Bristol**

Bristol City Council (1995) 'Travel to work data'

Bristol City Council (1997) 'North area profile – a statistical profile of North Bristol'

Bristol City Council (1998) 'Community Plan – North District' (draft)

Census Data 1981–91 *Housing Tenure.* ONS 1991 Census Small Area Statistics

Census Data 1981–91 *Travel to Work.* ONS 1991 Census Small Area Statistics

Census Data 1981–91 *Car Ownership*. ONS 1991 Census Small Area Statistics

## Case study: London Borough of Redbridge

London Borough of Redbridge (1995) *Housing Needs Study*. London: Chapman Hendy Associates

London Borough of Redbridge (1998) 'Economic Development Plan'

London Borough of Redbridge (1998) *1998 Residents' Survey*. London: RSGB

London Borough of Redbridge (1998) 'Strategy for Older People'

Redbridge Sustainability Panel (1998) *Redbridge into the 21st Century*. London: Redbridge LA21

## Case study: North Tyneside

Bellway Urban Renewal (together with the Guinness Trust, Howdon Gas Works) (1997) 'Feasibility Study for the site' (plan)

North Tyneside Council (1996) 'Unitary Development Plan – deposit draft'

North Tyneside Council (1997) Report on the provision of a replacement building for Stephenson Memorial First School and the redevelopment of the gas works site

North Tyneside Council (undated) 'Valuation: Howdon Gas Works site – Rosehill Road to Howdon Lane'

North Tyneside Council (undated) 'Site development conditions'

North Tyneside Council (1992) 'Survey of new housing'

North Tyneside Metropolitan Borough Council (undated) *Willington Quay Local Plan*.

Office of Population Censuses & Surveys, Census Data, 1981

TRL (Transport Research Laboratory, DETR) (by Davoudi S. *et al.*) (1993*) The Longer Term Effects of the Tyne and Wear Metro*. Crowthorne: TRL

TRRL (Transport and Road Research Laboratory, DETR) (by H. Lewis) (1985*) The Metro Report. The Impact of Metro and Public Transport Integration in Tyne and Wear*. Crowthorne: TRRL

TRRL (Transport and Road Research Laboratory, DETR) (by J.C Miles, C.G.B. Mitchell and K. Perrett) (1985) *Monitoring the effects of the Tyne and Wear Metro*. Crowthorne: TRRL

## Case study: Birmingham

Birmingham City Council (1990) 'Shenley Fields, an estate profile'

Birmingham City Council (1991) 'Report on Shenley Fields integrated area initiative major regeneration strategy'

Birmingham City Council (1993) 'Unitary development plan'

Birmingham City Council (1994) 'Egghill estate – draft area profile'

Birmingham City Council (1994) 'Northfield local action plan – draft'

Birmingham City Council (1995) 'Report on Ingoldsby estate regeneration'

Birmingham City Council (1995) 'Report on the West Northfield area regeneration initiative proposed strategy for the Bellfields area, Northfield'

Birmingham City Council (1995) 'West Northfield area regeneration initiative'

Birmingham City Council (1996) 'Report on the proposed housing strategy for the Egghill estate, Northfield'

Birmingham City Council (1997) 'Westcote Avenue Egghill estate, Northfield – draft development brief'

Birmingham City Council (undated) 'Brochure on Planning in Northfield'

Birmingham City Council (undated) 'Brochure on the West Northfield area regeneration initiative'

Birmingham City Council, Policy and Resources (West Northfield Area Regeneration Sub-committee) (March 1998) 'Report on the forward strategy for West Northfield'

Office of Population Censuses and Surveys, Census Data, 1991

Sullivan, H. (1997) *Report of the Evaluation of the Pilot Devolution Projects – West Northfield and Aston, Birmingham*. Institute of Local Government Studies, Birmingham University